W. S. (William Samuel) Gottheil

A Manual of General Histology

W. S. (William Samuel) Gottheil

A Manual of General Histology

ISBN/EAN: 9783742816887

Manufactured in Europe, USA, Canada, Australia, Japa

Cover: Foto ©ninafisch / pixelio.de

Manufactured and distributed by brebook publishing software (www.brebook.com)

W. S. (William Samuel) Gottheil

A Manual of General Histology

A MANUAL

OF

GENERAL HISTOLOGY

BY

WILLIAM S. GOTTHEIL, M.D.

PROFESSOR OF PATHOLOGY IN THE AMERICAN VETERINARY COLLEGE, NEW YORK;
PHYSICIAN TO THE LEBANON HOSPITAL, NEW YORK; FORMERLY SENIOR
LECTURER ON DERMATOLOGY AT THE NEW YORK POLICLINIC;
DERMATOLOGIST TO THE NORTHWESTERN AND THE
GERMAN WEST SIDE DISPENSARY, ETC.

Author of "A Manual of General Pathology"

FULLY ILLUSTRATED

NEW YORK
SABISTON, MURRAY & CO.
VETERINARY PUBLISHERS AND BOOKSELLERS
916 SIXTH AVENUE

1894

PREFACE.

HISTOLOGY is the basis of the Physician's art, as Anatomy is the foundation of the Surgeon's science. Only by knowing the processes of life can we understand the changes of disease and the actions of remedies. As the architect must know his building materials, so must the practitioner of medicine know the intimate structure of the body. No experience and no skill can entirely compensate him for the absence of this knowledge. He will not be able to see into the dense organs of the body, to watch their parts at work, to detect their deviations from normal standards, and to apply rational agents to influence them.

To present this knowledge in an accessible and simple form has been the author's task. Some considerable experience in teaching it to beginners has shown him the necessity of excluding theories and moot points, and of reducing the explanations of the structure of the body to their simplest possible terms. This, he trusts, he has in some degree accomplished.

January, 1894.

CONTENTS.

INTRODUCTION,	The Cell,	1
PART I.	The Simple Tissues,	10
CHAPTER I.	Blood and Lymph,	10
CHAPTER II.	Epithelium and Endothelium,	15
CHAPTER III.	The Connective Substances,	20
	Mucoid Tissue,	21
CHAPTER IV.	The Connective Substances (Cont'd),	23
	White Fibrous Tissue,	23
	Yellow Elastic Tissue,	25
CHAPTER V.	The Connective Substances (Cont'd),	27
	Fatty Tissue,	27
	Cartilage,	29
CHAPTER VI.	The Connective Substances (Cont'd),	33
	Bone,	33
CHAPTER VII.	The Muscular Tissue,	40
	Unstriped Muscle,	40
	Striated Muscle,	42
	Cardiac Muscle,	45

CONTENTS.

Chapter VIII.	The Nervous Tissue, .	46
	Nerve Fibres, .	46
	Nerve Cells, .	53
Part II. The Compound Tissues, .		55
Chapter IX.	The Vessels, .	55
	The Bloodvessels,	55
	The Lymph Vessels, .	58
Chapter X.	Membranes, .	59
	Mucous Membranes, .	59
	Serous Membranes, .	61
	Synovial Membranes,	61
Part III. The Organs,		63
Chapter XI.	The Glands, .	63
	Lymphatic Glands, .	63
	Salivary Glands,	66
	The Pancreas, .	68
	The Mammary Gland,	68
Chapter XII.	The Glands (Continued),	71
	The Spleen,	71
	The Liver,	74
Chapter XIII.	The Alimentary Canal,	78
	The Teeth,	78
	The Mouth,	80
	The Tongue, .	81
	The Œsophagus,	83

CONTENTS.

Chapter XIV.	The Alimentary Canal (Continued),	84
	The Stomach,	84
	The Small Intestine,	87
	The Large Intestine,	90
Chapter XV.	The Respiratory System,	92
	The Larynx,	92
	The Trachea,	93
	The Bronchi,	93
	The Lungs,	95
Chapter XVI.	The Urinary System,	98
	The Kidneys,	98
	The Ureters,	104
	The Bladder,	104
	The Urethra,	105
Chapter XVII.	The Male Genital Organs,	106
	The Testis,	106
	The Epididymis,	109
	The Prostate,	110
	The Penis,	110
Chapter XVIII.	The Female Genital Organs,	112
	The Ovary,	112
	The Uterus,	116
	The Fallopian Tubes,	117
	The Vagina,	117
	Nymphæ, Clitoris and Vestibulum,	117

CHAPTER XIX.	The Skin,	118
	The Nails,	122
	The Hairs,	122
CHAPTER XX.	The Eye,	126
CHAPTER XXI.	The Central Nervous System,	133
	The Spinal Cord,	133
	The Brain,	136

A Manual of General Histology.

INTRODUCTION.

The Cell.

OUR accurate knowledge of the constitution of organic bodies is only of recent date. Prior to the labors of Schleiden in the vegetable world, and of Schwann upon animals, our ideas of the intimate methods of the life processes of living beings were of the crudest possible kind. The elder physiologists and anatomists had indeed a general knowledge of the grosser phenomena of life; but their minute nature was unknown to them.

When, therefore, Schwann discovered the true structure of the animal tissues, a new era began for all these sciences that are concerned with the constitutions and functions, normal and abnormal, of the animal body. A flood of light was thrown into a thousand dark places, and undreamed of fields of investigation were revealed. An impetus was given to Biology and Medicine and all their subsidiary sciences, the result of which has been the brilliant achievements of the last half century.

The fact that Schwann proclaimed was this : *That every animal tissue is built up of an immense number of minute bodies, each one of which is a complete organic being, and capable of all those things which together we call life.* These minute living bodies are the *cells.*

Constitution of cells.—Most cells consist of three distinct parts. First we have the *cell body*, usually semi-fluid ; then the *cell wall*, of a harder and more resistant material ; then the *nucleus*, placed inside the body, and generally round in shape ; and finally, still another minute body, inside the nucleus, called the *nucleolus.* The earlier investigators believed that all these parts were essential for the complete cell, and so great an authority as Virchow supported them. But exceptions were soon noticed and the definition had to be modified. The nucleolus certainly was not essential. Many cells never showed a nucleolus at all ; others showed it at certain stages of growth only. Then cells were found in which no cell wall could be demonstrated, as in those of blood and pus, in embryonic and other cells. Finally animal cells were found by Stricker, Brücke and others, in which the nucleus itself was absent.

Thus neither nucleus, nucleolus, nor cell wall were necessary. A little mass of living matter could exhibit all the properties of the complete cell.

The body of the cell, this mass of living matter, is composed of a substance which Max Schultze first called *Protoplasm*. It is the essential portion of the cell, the real living tissue, and is the same substance that Beale calls *Bioplasm.*

Protoplasm is an albuminoid body, closely related to the other albuminous proximate principles of the

THE CELL.

animal body, albuminose, caseine, etc.; being, in fact, the original substance from which the other members of the group are derived. It is insoluble in water, and coagulates at death. It is a more or less viscid, semi-solid, structureless and homogeneous substance.

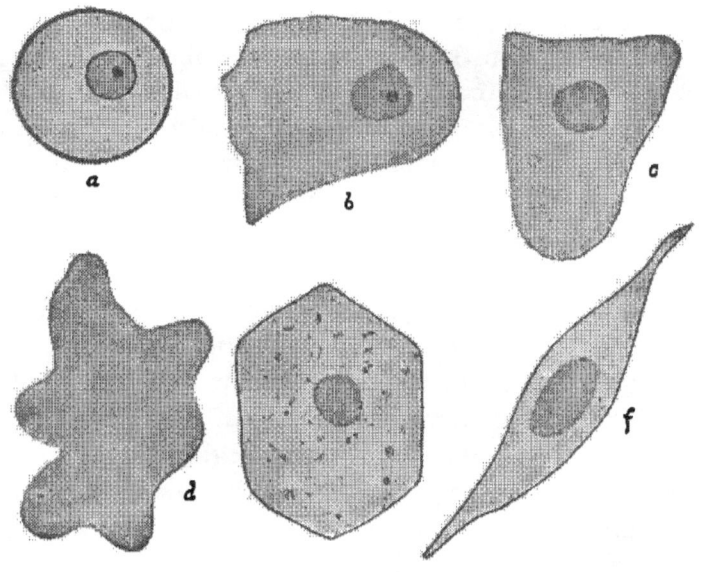

FIG. 1.—Cells.

a, Schematic Cell with Cell-wall, Nucleus, and Nucleolus. b, Cell without Wall. c, Cell without Wall or Nucleolus. d, Cell without Wall, Nucleus, or Nucleolus. e, f, Other Forms of Cells.

Water causes it to swell up, and ultimately disintegrates it; so do dilute acids and alkalies. After the death of the cell it may become transformed into other members of the albuminoid group. Thus is formed the hard *Keratin* of the nails and horns from the protoplasm of the epithelial cells; and thus also *Mucin, Albuminose*, etc., are produced.

The *cell body* varies much in shape; it may be spherical, ovoid, fusiform, cuboidal, or scale-like, or it may be quite irregular in shape; crystals, drops of fat and pigment-granules are frequently imbedded in its substance.

The *cell wall* when present is simply the hardened outer layer of the protoplasmic body of the cell.

The *nucleus* in the adult cell is a spherical or irregular body, often coarsely granular and containing a filiform net-work. Its size varies greatly in proportion to the cell. It is usually single; but some cells are multi-nucleated, especially in young and rapidly growing tissues; whilst others, such as the red corpuscles of the blood, have lost their original nucleus entirely. Not only is the nucleus more resistant to disease and injury than the rest of the cell, but it also takes up staining agents more readily, and is evidently denser than the general protoplasm of the cells.

The size of cells varies considerably; a small red blood corpuscle may measure only $\frac{1}{18000}$ of an inch (Java musk deer); whilst a large spinal ganglion cell (man) reaches a size of $\frac{1}{180}$ of an inch.

All animals are composed of immense numbers of such cells, and they are so intimately related to, and bound up with one another that it becomes difficult to study their properties to advantage. But there exist some animals so low in the organic scale that their bodies are composed of but a single cell; and these we can examine under the microscope, and study under favorable conditions. It thus becomes possible to describe the life-history and the functions of a single cell, and to determine the part played in them by its various portions, cell wall, protoplasm, and nucleus.

Such a simple animal is the *Amoeba*, of which many varieties are known to biologists, and which closely resemble the white blood corpuscles of vertebrates. The amoeba consists of a simple, undifferentiated mass of protoplasm, sometimes without even a cell wall. Yet it shows all the phenomena of life. It eats, moves, assimilates, and reproduces. It is Life reduced to its simplest terms of expression. It is a simple living cell, and its study will reveal to us the properties of the minute structures that compose the organic body.

Now the amoeba, a single cell composed of undifferentiated protoplasm, shows the following fundamental properties :

1st, *Contractility*.—The amoeba moves ; careful examination shows us that it changes its position. A minute projection appears at one side of the protoplasmic mass ; this gradually grows larger and larger, the material of the cell flowing from its body into the projection. Finally the entire cell has followed ; and the organism has moved away from its original location.

2d, *Irritability and Automatic Action*.—Any disturbance of the amoeba causes action. A push against it, not only displaces it, as it would an inanimate body ; it causes a manifestation of energy on the part of the animal. This is usually made apparent by motion ; but it might show itself by heat production, or in other ways. The amoeba is irritable because an irritant causes it to *move of itself*.

But it is also automatic ; it may move without external irritation, the stimulus coming from within the body of the animal. The amoeba moves when stimulated from without or from within, as do the higher animals.

3d, *Assimilation.*—The amoeba takes in food and digests it. We can see it gradually move towards some foreign particle and, flowing around it, at length enclose it within its own body. There such portions of the foreign body as are fit for food are retained and digested; whilst the unfit portions are cast out by the amoeba flowing away from them. The portions retained become part of the body of the cell.

4th, *Metabolism.*—Chemical change (metabolism) is constantly going on in the amoeba. Not only are other substances taken into its body changed into protoplasm and added to it, so that the amoeba grows; but its own protoplasm undergoes a retrograde change and is cast out when used up. As in the higher animals, when young the amoeba takes in more material than it casts off, it grows; when adult, equilibrium is established; and when old the amount of waste exceeds the amount taken in. The energy that supplies the stimulus for the other life processes is also metabolic in its origin.

5th, *Respiration.*—This is essentially the taking in of oxygen into the body as a food. The amoeba needs oxygen; it must be present in the material in which it floats. It promptly dies when placed in a medium that does not contain it. It also excretes the products of oxidation, as carbonic acid. Hence, in the same sense as in the higher animals, the amoeba breathes.

6th, *Reproduction.*—As new material is taken in and added to the amoeba it increases in size. Finally there comes a time when it divides, and each portion becomes a complete individual. This process of reproduction may consist of a simple *Division*, the cell splitting through all its parts. Or *Vacuolation* may occur, a hollow space appearing in the interior of the cell, and new cells growing into it from the protoplasm or nucleus of the old one, which latter finally ruptures, and sets the young cells free. *Gemmation* is a rarer method; buds spring out from the body of the cell and, becoming detached, form new individuals. Thus the single-celled amoeba reproduces its like from the materials of its own body as the higher animals do.

These are the properties exhibited by the amoeba; and they are exactly those that constitute the functions of life in all animals. For all animals are simply groups of amoebæ associated together. And since the whole cannot exhibit any properties fundamentally different from those of its component parts, the complex phenomena of organic life are simply modifications of the primative functions of the original cells. The ovum is this original cell of animal life; from it all the others are derived, both in substance and in function.

Now in the course of evolution of organic life the same thing has come to pass that has happened in the evolution of social life. As primeval man did everything for himself, so the original cell has in itself all the functions of life. As each civilized man can do a few things much better than most other civilized men, and infinitely better than an uncivilized man, so in the complex organic structure of the higher animals certain cells are specialized for certain work. The principle is that of the *Division of Labor;* special aptitudes and special powers come from undivided attention to certain things. Certain groups of animal cells are set apart early in the development of the body to do especially one or other of the primitive functions described above. And whilst in so doing they become more or less altered in structure, forming the various kinds of cells that histology shows us, they also acquire enhanced powers in their special functions, so that these latter may appear to be almost new properties.

Such a group of cells with some special work to do and with some special differences of structure in consequence thereof, is called a *Tissue*. A certain amount of uniting material called *Intercellular Substance* binds the cells of a tissue into one mass. Those tissues in which the property of contractility is marked are called muscles; those which are especially irritable and automatic form the nervous tissues; those which are specially concerned in reproduction form the reproductive tissues; and so on. Hence we may classify the tissues as follows:

1st, *The contractile tissues;* the muscles.

2d, *The irritable and automatic tissues;* the nerves.

3d, *The metabolic and secretory tissues;* the hepatic cells, the digestive and urinary epithelium, etc.

4th, *The respiratory tissues;* the pulmonary epithelium.

5th, *The reproductive tissues;* the ovary and testis.

6th, *The indifferent and mechanical tissues;* cartilage, bone, etc.

But although certain groups of cells are thus set apart to do certain kinds of work and perhaps in the normal state do nothing but that work, the other properties and functions of the original cell are only in the background and in abeyance; they are not absent.

Under certain conditions cells may exhibit properties different from their usual ones. Thus nerve cells and muscle cells, though primarily concerned with sensation and motion, may reproduce when injured; so that a nerve or muscle divided and then united aseptically may be repaired by the formation of new nerve or muscle cells. Though certain epithelial cells are busied with the work of assimilation, all the cells of the body assimilate to a greater or less degree. So do all the tissues retain more or less metabolic power; they each one possess the power of inducing chemical change in the substances they take up, though that function is the especial province of the hepatic, the gastro-intestinal epithelial cells, etc. It is especially under conditions of disease and injury that these subsidiary functions are brought into prominence.

PART I.

THE SIMPLE TISSUES.

The Simple Tissues are the anatomical elements out of which the body is built. In some cases they occur alone; but in most instances they are combined together to form the more complicated structures.

CHAPTER I.

BLOOD AND LYMPH.

Blood is a tissue composed of cells in a fluid intercellular substance. The cells are of three kinds, red blood corpuscles, white or colorless blood corpuscles (leucocytes), and free granules.

The *red blood corpuscles*. These bodies, which give the blood its peculiar color, are homogeneous, biconcave, disc-shaped cells, without nucleus, or cell wall; seen singly they have a yellowish tint, but when crowded together in great numbers they give the familiar deep red color to the blood. They vary greatly in size in different animals, thus: man, $\frac{1}{3200}$ in.; cat, $\frac{1}{4000}$ in.; horse, $\frac{1}{4600}$ in.; sheep, $\frac{1}{5000}$ in.;

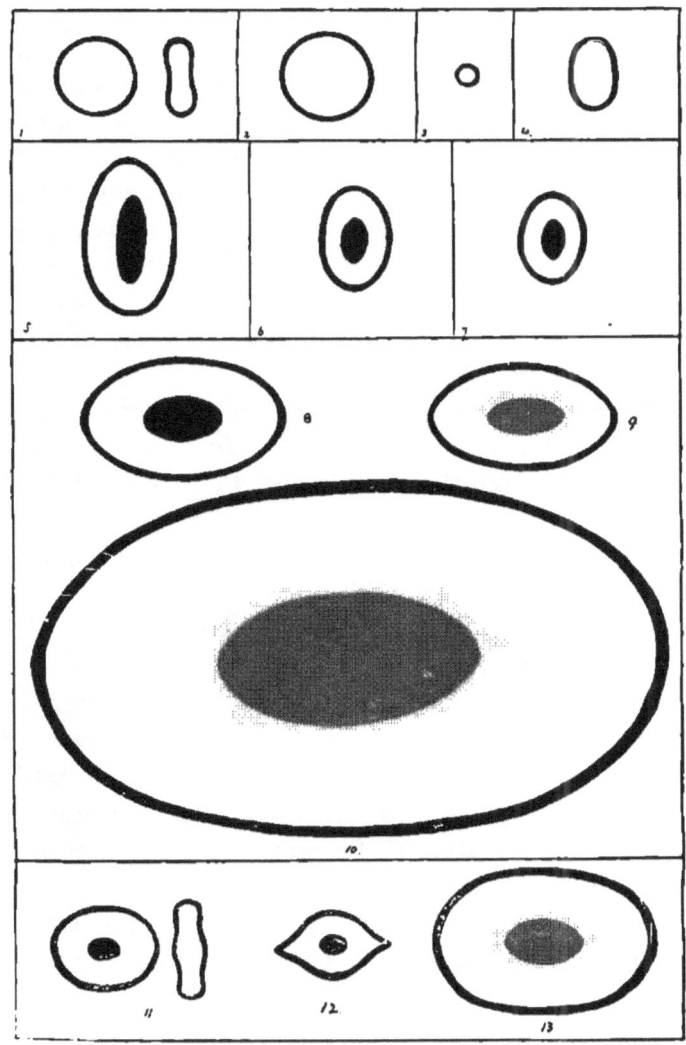

Fig. 2.—Comparative Sizes of Red Blood Corpuscles.

1, Man. 2, Elephant. 3, Java Musk Deer. 4, Dromedary. 5, Ostrich. 6, Pigeon, 7, Humming-bird. 8, Crocodile. 9, Python. 10, Proteus. 11, Perch. 12, Pike. 13, Shark. (Carpenter.)

elephant, $\frac{1}{2740}$ in.; musk deer, $\frac{1}{12000}$ in.; toad, $\frac{1}{1013}$ in.; newt, $\frac{1}{817}$ in.; proteus, $\frac{1}{460}$ in. Their shape is circular in all mammals except the camellidæ, in which it is oval. In non-mammalians it may be round or oval, but is usually large, and always nucleated.

Mixed with water, the red blood cells swell up, and their coloring matter is dissolved out of them. From their peculiar shape, they tend to stick together in rouleaux; they are by far the most abundant of the blood cells, there being five hundred of them to one white cell, or free granule.

The color of the red cells is due to the presence of a crystallizable substance called *Hæmoglobin;* when blood escapes from the vessels and lies diffused in the tissues, the coloring matter leaves the cells and crystalizes in certain forms which vary with the animal to whom the blood belongs.

The *white or colorless blood corpuscles* differ but little in size in different animals, being about $\frac{1}{3000}$ of an inch in diameter. They are composed of a granular protoplasm containing one or more nuclei and some fat granules; being, in fact, amoebæ moving and taking in food, exactly as described in the Introduction.

These white cells are of great importance in many normal and pathological processes.

Free granules. These are small bodies usually globular in shape, and only one-third to one-half the size of the red blood cells. We know but little about them, though it is probable that they play an important part in certain disease processes.

The *intercellular substance* of the blood is a homogeneous fluid substance called *plasma.* It is entirely structureless during life.

The red corpuscle probably arises in the spleen, or in the red marrow of the bones, whilst the white corpuscles appear to be derived from the lymphatic organs.

Microscopic examination of the blood is of the greatest importance from a medico-legal point of view, since on the determination whether certain stains are

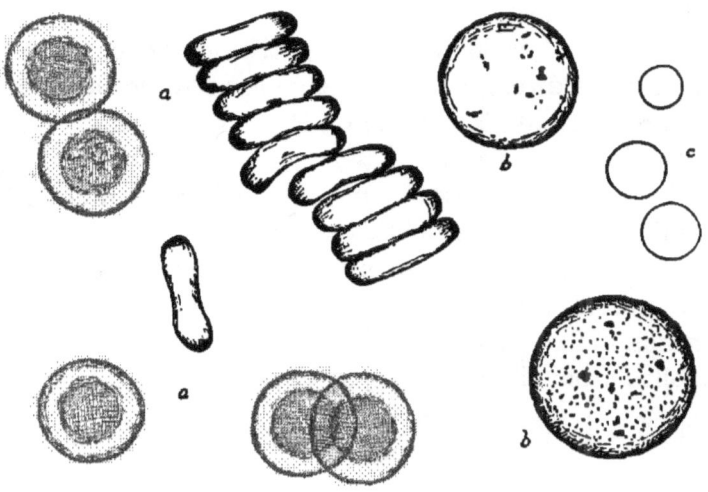

Fig. 3—Human Blood Cells.

a, Red Blood Corpuscles, Single and in Rouleaux. b, White Blood Cells. c, Blood Granules or Discs.

the remains of human blood or not may frequently depend a human life. The limits within which this can be done are well known, although incompetent expert testimony upon the subject is the rule rather than the exception. The following facts will guide us. First, it is impossible to say that any given blood specimen is positively human blood. The blood cells of many common animals, the horse, sheep, dog, cat, etc., cannot be distinguished from the red cell of human blood. Second, certain red blood cells can positively be said *not* to be of human origin ; oval cells, non-nucleated, come from the camel tribe ; oval cells, nucleated, come from some non-mammalian animal. Third, cells very large or very small may be identified positively as not belonging to man or the ordinary domestic animals.

On the other hand, the negative evidence may be much more direct, as it may enable us to decide that a certain specimen is not the bird's or the reptile's blood that it is claimed to be.

Lymph is a tissue composed of spheroidal cells identical in structure with the white blood cells, a few red cells, and a varying number of minute globules. The intercellular substance is identical with the blood plasma. The lymph globules are in no way distinguished from the white blood cells.

CHAPTER II.

EPITHELIUM AND ENDOTHELIUM.

THE Epithelium is the tissue covering the external surfaces of the body, both dermal and mucous, and lining the glandular structures connected with them. Its cells are protective and secreting. It is composed of large nucleated cells, with a small amount of intercellular substance to cement them together. Two chief varieties occur, in accordance with the two chief functions of the tissue.

Surface or Covering Epithelium is found as the upper layer of the skin and the mucous membranes. Its cells are large and flat, with prominent nuclei, and are united at their edges to form continuous membranes. Hair, nails, and horns are composed of modified epithelium cells of this variety.

Glandular Epithelium is found in the various secreting structures of the body, as in the glands of the intestinal tract, the skin, etc. The cells are more or less column-shaped, with large oval nuclei, and a longitudinally striated protoplasm.

16   A MANUAL OF GENERAL HISTOLOGY.

The size of the epithelial cells varies much, even in the same tissue ; in general it is from $\frac{1}{1500}$ to $\frac{1}{500}$ of an inch. There may be only a single layer, or there may be a number of stratified layers either of columnar or of scale-like cells. We therefore have :

1st, *Pavement Epithelium*, consisting of flattened cells, which may be *Simple*, as in the lung saccules

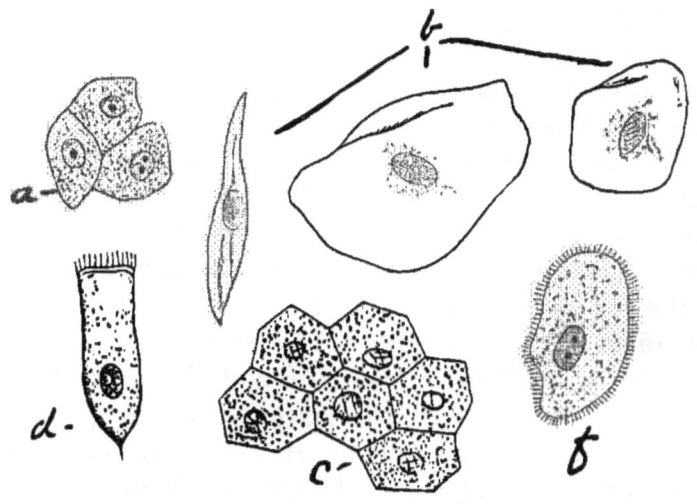

FIG. 4.—Epithelial Cells.

a, Pavement Epithelium. b, Squamous Epithelium of Mouth. c, Polyhedral Epithelium from Retina d, Ciliated Conical Epithelium from Trachea. f, Prickle Cells.

and the inactive mammary gland ; or *Stratified*, as in the external mucosæ and the skin.

2d, *Columnar Epithelium*, consisting of prismatic cells laid side by side, their tops forming free surfaces. This also may be *Simple*, as in the uriniferous tubules ; or *Compound*, as in the stomach and intestines.

EPITHELIUM AND ENDOTHELIUM.

Certain other varieties may be mentioned. *Ciliated Epithelium* is usually columnar, and is peculiar in that its free surface is provided with a number of minute prolongations or hairs, called cilia, which are apparently continuous with striæ of the cell protoplasm and nucleus. These cilia are in continuous, rapid, and whip-like synchronous motion during life, and are found in situations where a definite direction to certain material is required. In the Fallopian tube their motion is from the fimbriated extremity towards

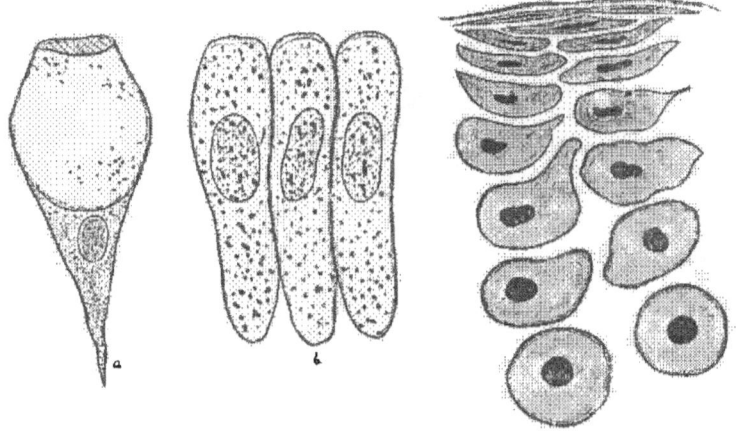

FIG. 5.—Epithelium.

a. Goblet Cell. *b,* Columnar Epithelium. *c,* Stratified Epithelium of the Cornea, showing the gradual flattening as they reach the surface.

the uterus, thus probably helping the ovum on in its course; in the efferent ducts of the testicle the current is from within outwards, thus aiding the excretion of the semen. The *Prickle Cells* are irregular epithelial cells of the pavement variety with cilia all over their surfaces. They are found in the middle and deeper

18   A MANUAL OF GENERAL HISTOLOGY.

layers of the skin. *Goblet Cells* grow in the epithelium of the stomach, the intestines, and the respiratory tract. They are ordinary columnar cells in the glandular structures of these organs, and are swelled out into goblet shape by the material secreted from their own substance and destined to be excreted on the surface. *Pigment Cells* are epithelial cells filled with black pigment crystals. They form the dark colors of the choroid and the iris, and are present in the skin.

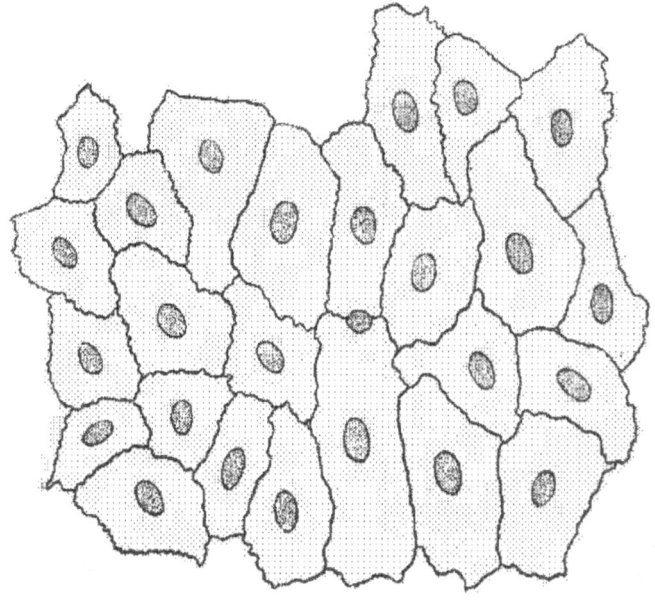

FIG. 6.—Endothelium of a Serous Membrane. (Schaefer.)

Epithelial cells grow by division. This is especially marked in the stratified pavement epithelium, where the upper layers either dry up and become horny and are cast off, as in the skin, or are macerated and removed in the fluids of the part, as is the case in the mucous membranes. The deeper layers are being continuously multiplied by division, and pushed up in their place.

Endothelium differs in no way from epithelium, save that it lines the internal closed cavities of the body. The cells are always of the simple pavement variety, and are united together by an intercellular cement. Endothelium composes the outer layer of the serous membranes, thus lining the internal cavities of the body, the peritoneal, pleural, and pericardial cavities, and that of the bloodvessels.

CHAPTER III.

THE CONNECTIVE SUBSTANCES.

THESE are the tissues whose function is the supporting of the body. There are a number of different varieties; but they are similar in structure, and are all derived from one embryonic source, the middle blasto-dermic layer. They are interchangeable, one variety becoming another in the course of development, and also in certain pathological processes. They all consist of cells and intercellular substance; but whilst the cells are much alike, the intercellular substance varies greatly in amount and constitution.

The following are the chief varieties of the connective substance:

1st, *Mucoid or Embryonic Connective Tissue.*
2d, *White Fibrous Connective Tissue.*
3d, *Yellow Elastic Connective Tissue.*
4th, *Fatty Tissue.*
5th, *Cartilage.*
6th, *Bone.*

THE CONNECTIVE SUBSTANCES.

There are other varieties, or rather sub-varieties, of the above classes, such as Tendon, Adenoid tissue, Areolar tissue, Reticulated tissue, Dentine, etc.

The cells of the connective substances have different varieties, being called bone cells, connective tissue corpuscles, tendon cells, cartilage cells, or fat cells, as the case may be. The intercellular substance yields, on chemical treatment, Collagen, Gelatine,

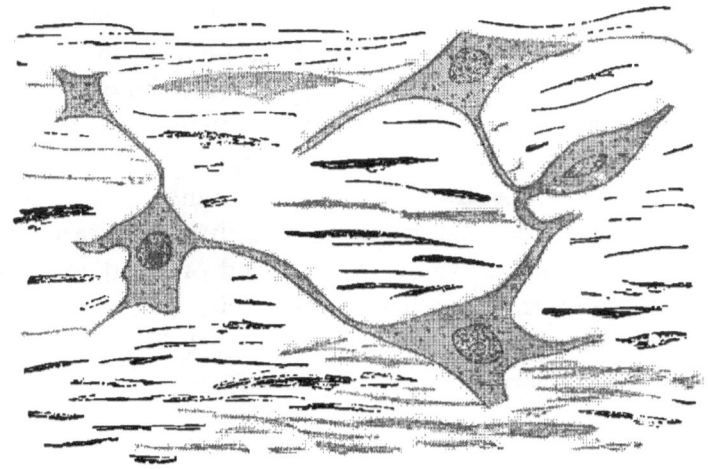

FIG. 7.—Mucoid Tissue. Intercellular Substance becoming slightly fibrillated.

Chondrin, etc., all closely allied; which we shall describe more minutely when we consider the varieties of the substance.

Mucoid Tissue.

This tissue, known also as *Embryonic* or *Gelatinous Connective Tissue*, is the simplest and the original form of the connective substance, and the one from which the others are derived. All the various connective substances are laid down first in the fœtus in this embryonal shape, before they reach their perfected forms. At birth it is still found in the umbilical cord, where it forms the Jelly of Wharton; in the adult it does not exist save in a much changed form, as the vitreous humor of the eye; and it also occurs in certain tumors.

Mucoid tissue consists of cells in a semi-fluid intercellular substance. The cells at first are round, but in later stages become spindle-shaped, branched or irregular; they also diminish in number as compared with the intercellular substance. Mucoid tissue in its latest stages shows but a few long spindle cells. The intercellular substance at first is homogeneous and structureless; in later forms it is slightly fibrillated.

All varieties of shape of cell and of fibrillation of the intercellular substance are met with as the mucoid tissue gradually changes into the more highly developed forms of the connective substances.

CHAPTER IV.

THE CONNECTIVE SUBSTANCES. (*Continued.*)

White Fibrous Connective Tissue or Fibrous Tissue.

THIS is the connective tissue par excellence, and is found in every organ and portion of the body. It forms the mass of the skin, the mucous membranes, tendons, fasciæ, ligaments, etc. It is the great supporter of the body, binding the bones together, dividing and enclosing muscles and nerves, and forming the framework upon which is placed all the cellular elements of the internal organs; so that if every other element could be removed from an animal body a complete image of the shape of all the parts would be left behind in white fibrous connective tissue. It is derived from the mucoid tissue of the embryo.

Fibrous tissue consists of cells and a complex intercellular substance. The cells vary much in size and shape in different structures. In tendons and fasciæ they are elongated, flattened and slenderly nucleated bodies. In serous membranes they are flat and irreg-

24 A MANUAL OF GENERAL HISTOLOGY.

ular, with many branches, and a round nucleus. In the skin they are of entirely irregular shape. When the cells are fusiform they are collected into gray translucent bundles, which may be placed parallel to one another as to form tendons or crossed as to form membranes or networks. These fasciculi vary much in size. The intercellular substance is fibrillated

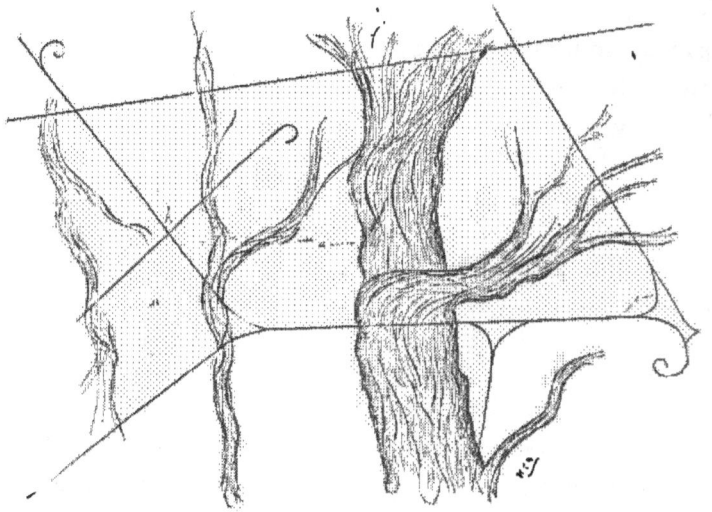

FIG. 8.—White Fibrous Connective Tissue.
a, White Fibrous Tissue. *b*, Elastic Fibres.

and is large in amount. The cells are frequently so compressed and hidden by it as to be barely visible. It yields globulin to chemical action.

Sub-varieties of the white fibrous connective tissue are the following :

1st, *Reticulated Tissue*. Here the connective-tissue bundles are so placed as to form a reticulum or network, as in the skin.

2d, *Adenoid Tissue.* Very similar to reticulated tissue. It forms the framework of the lymphatic glands.

3d, *Neuroglia*, which is the peculiar fibrous-tissue framework that supports the nerve cells of the brain.

4th, *Tendon Tissue*, in which the fibrous-tissue cells are arranged in closely aggregated bundles.

5th, *Corneal Tissue*, with large multi-branched connective-tissue cells.

5th, *Pigmentary Connective Tissue*, where branched connective-tissue cells are largely filled with black or brown pigment grains. These are most prominent in amphibia and reptiles, in whom they cause the peculiar coloration of the skin ; in man they are only found in the iris and choroid.

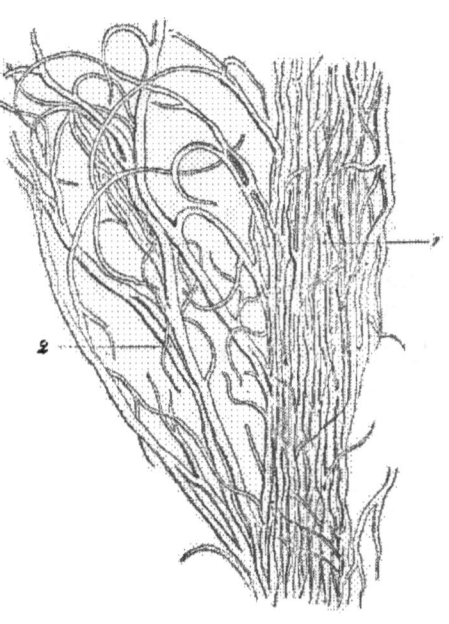

FIG. 9.—Yellow Elastic Connective Tissue.
1, Elastic Fibres in their natural position.
2, The same teased apart. (Morel.)

Yellow Elastic Connective Tissue.

This variety usually occurs in conjunction with other members of the same group, more or less of it being found in all the fibrous tissues. The alveoli of the lung, the endocardium and the cardiac valves, the ligamentum flava, contain large quantities of it ; whilst in the largest blood vessels, as the aorta, and in the ligamentum nuchæ, it is found almost pure.

No cells have yet been demonstrated in yellow elactic connective tissue. It is composed of thick, bright, yellow, dividing, anastomotic fibres, arranged as a network, or scattered through other connective tissues. The fibres are often twisted, and curl up strongly at their torn ends on account of their great elasticity. Their size, marked yellow color, and resiliency render them easily distinguishable in the other tissues. They yield, not gelatine, but elasticine.

Yellow elastic tissue is found wherever in the body elasticity and strength combined are required.

CHAPTER V.

THE CONNECTIVE SUBSTANCES. (*Continued.*)

Fatty Tissue.

FATTY Tissue is an ordinary white fibrous connective tissue with very little intercellular substance and in which much of the body of the connective-tissue cells has been swollen by fat. Such a cell appears to be composed simply of a large globule of fat; the globules being arranged in clusters separated by partitions of fibrous connective tissue. The blood and lymph vessels run in these inter-cluster partitions. The cell, however, is always present. Part of its protoplasm at least remains, as does the cell wall and the nucleus; but they are disposed in a very thin layer around the central globule of fat and are not visible on casual inspection.

The manner in which fatty tissue develops during growth and fattening, and the manner in which it disappears during emaciation will help us to understand its peculiar structure. The tissues that are to be fat are laid down as ordinary mucoid tissue in the fœtus. Then there appear in the cell bodies minute shining particles which gradually coalesce to form droplets of fat. The growing fat globule crowds the

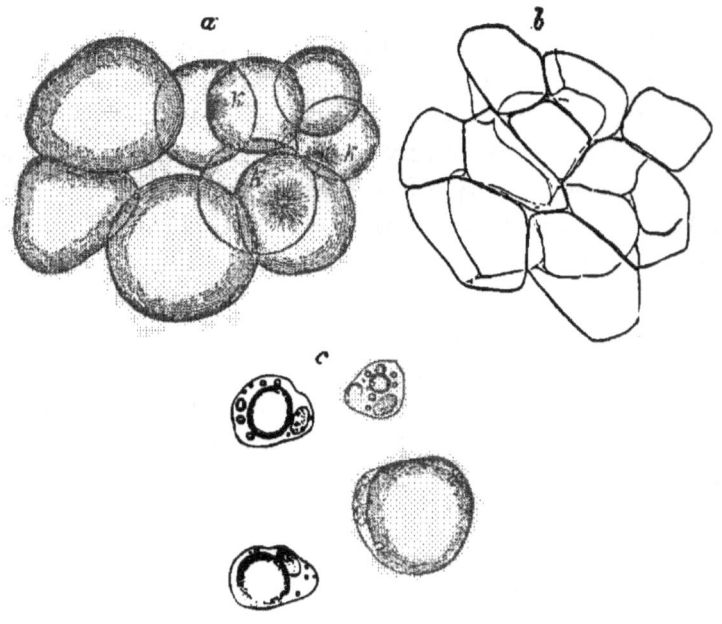

Fig. 10.—Fatty Tissue.

a, Normal Fat Cells from the Panniculus Adiposus; at *k*, Fat Crystals. *b*, Fat Cells with oil removed. *c*, Process of the removal of the oil from Fat Cells.

nucleus and the protoplasm of the cell to one side until finally the fusiform cell has become a large globe apparently composed of fat alone.

In the wasting diseases and during starvation the exact reverse of this process occurs. As the fat is removed the globule shrinks, and nucleus and cell body become apparent. The cell loses its globular shape and tends to become oval or fusiform. Soon a few drops of fat only remain and when these disappear the cell returns to its original state. Hence the fatty substance is always an infiltration and in no way injures the connective-tissue cell itself.

Cartilage.

Cartilage is a translucent, bluish-white tissue composed of connective-tissue cells in a basement substance that yields chondrin when boiled.

It is covered with a membrane called *Perichondrium* wherever it presents a free surface; and this membrane contains the vessels, nerves, etc., of the cartilage. The cells vary considerably in shape, but are most often triangular, though they may be spheroidal or flat. They contain one or two large nuclei, and their protoplasm is often granular. A distinct capsule encloses the cell, being composed merely of a hardened layer of the basement substance. When exposed to the air the cells shrink, leaving a space between their borders and the capsule wall.

The intercellular substance differs even more than do the cells, and upon this difference is based the classification of cartilage into three main varieties. These varieties are: Hyaline Cartilage, Fibro-cartilage, and Elastic Cartilage.

Cartilage itself contains neither vessels nor nerves, nor lymphatics; these structures are in the perichondrium and from it the tissue is nourished and enervated.

1st, *Hyaline Cartilage*. This is found in the articular ends of the long bones, in the costal cartilages,

30   A MANUAL OF GENERAL HISTOLOGY.

the tracheal and bronchial rings, the septum nasi, the laryngeal cartilages, etc. The cells are spherical or oval, with one or two nuclei, and are situated in distinct lacunæ in the basement substance. Each lacuna is lined by a delicate membrane which forms

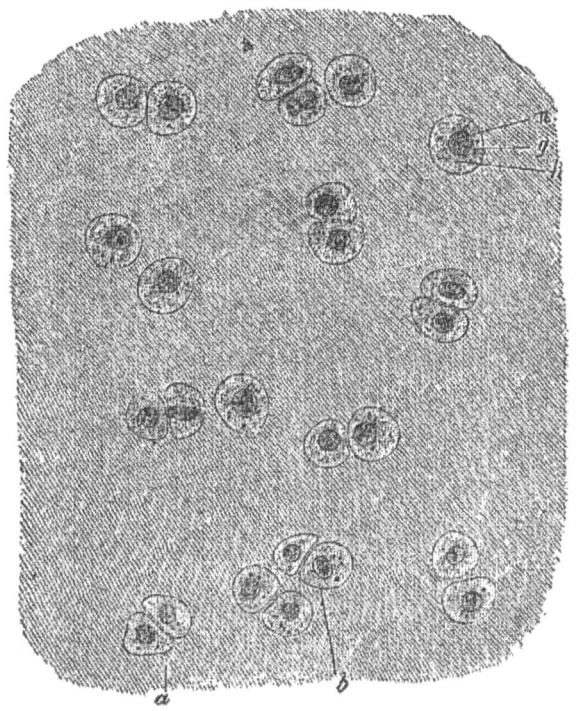

FIG. 11.—Hyaline Cartilage.

a, b, Groups of Cells.   *h,* Protoplasm of Cell.   *g,* Fatty Granules.
n, Nucleus.

the capsule; which, however, is only a slightly differentiated layer of the basement substance.

The intercellular substance of hyaline cartilage is characteristic. It is a transparent, firm, glassy, and structureless substance. Very thin sections are transparent; thicker ones are like ground glass; and still thicker layers are opalescent.

The hyaline cartilage cells frequently contain drops of fat and dark granules of lime salts. Calcification often occurs in it, and is a part of the process by which the cartilage becomes bone.

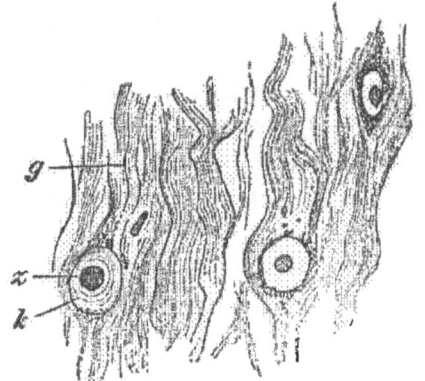

FIG. 12.—Fibro-Cartilage.

2d, *Fibro-cartilage* is a fibrous connective-tissue cartilage, *i. e.*, cartilage cells in a groundwork of white fibrous connective tissue. The cells do not differ in any way from those of the hyaline variety. But the intercellular substance is composed of ordinary white fibrous connective tissue, arranged in bundles. In the fully developed fibro-cartilage it is very small in amount. Fibro-cartilage is found in the inter-vertebral discs and the inter-articular cartilages.

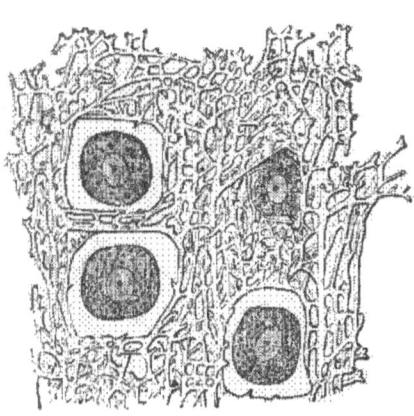

FIG. 12a.—Elastic Cartilage.

3d. *Elastic Cartilage* or yellow cartilage consists of cartilage cells in a groundwork of yellow elastic connective-tissue fibres. It occurs in the epiglottis, the external ear, the laryngeal cartilages of Wrisberg and Santorini, etc. The cells are of the ordinary cartilage variety, but the basis substance is largely interspersed with yellow elastic fibres. More or less white fibrous tissue and hyaline substance is always present, and the amount of elastic fibre varies greatly.

CHAPTER VI.

THE CONNECTIVE SUBSTANCES. (*Continued.*)

Bone.

BONE is a connective tissue in which the basement substance is impregnated with lime salts.

Two-thirds of its mass is earthy, and only one-third animal substance; and hence arises the hardness and tenacity of bone. The lime salts are chiefly on the form of phosphate of lime. It is possible to separate these two parts of bone one from the other. If we immerse a bone in an acid solution of the proper strength, we will in the course of time dissolve out all the mineral matter, leaving only the animal tissue behind. Such a decalcified bone has the shape and size of the natural bone; but it is translucent and, above all, perfectly soft and pliable. It can be bent and tied into a knot, all the material that gives bone its rigidity and brittleness having been removed. On the other hand if a bone is exposed to the action of fire for a sufficient time the animal matter can be burnt out of it, leaving only the mineral matter behind. Such a bone is of normal size and shape, but snow white and extremely friable; it falls to dust at the slightest touch. The intimate union of the two materials gives to the tissue its peculiar properties.

Bone is met with in two forms in the animal body : as *Compact Bone*, and as *Cancellated Bone*. Compact bone is the ordinary material known to us as forming

FIG. 13.—Transverse Section of Bone.

Showing Haversian Canals with Lamellæ around them, with Lacunæ and Canaliculi.

the shafts of the long bones, and the outer layer of the flat and irregular bones. It is a dense ivory-like substance, capable of being carved and polished. Cancellated bone on the other hand, is found in the interior of the flat bones, and in the heads of the long

THE CONNECTIVE SUBSTANCES. 35

bones. It is a honeycomb-like or spongy structure, the interstices of which are filled with marrow.

Bone, like the other connective substances, is composed of cells and intercellular substance. The *bone cells* or *bone corpuscles* are irregular, nucleated, multi-branched cells, which are arranged in the hard intercellular substance in a certain definite order. It we make a thin section of a piece of hard bone, we can see that it is studded with a number of irregularly round openings, around which the bone cells are arranged in concentric layers. These round openings are known as *Haversian*

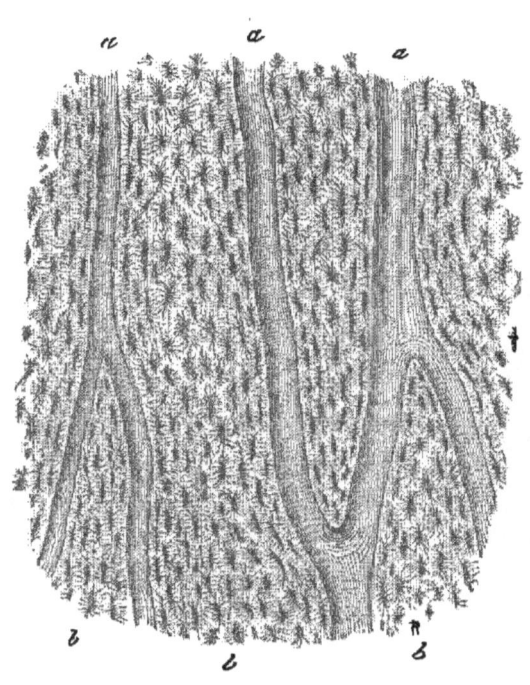

FIG. 14.—Longitudinal Section of Bone.

a, Haversian Canals. *b*, Lacunæ and Canaliculi. (Sappey.)

Canals, from Clopton Havers, a distinguished English physician of the seventeenth century who first described them. They are the channels in which run the blood-vessels of bone, together with its lymphatics and nerves. Running lengthwise as they do through the hard bone, they are seen as circular openings in ordinary transverse sections; and appear as long, branched canals in longitudinal sections.

Around each Haversian canal are several concentric rows of irregular spaces with minute branches and channels communicating one with another and with the central Haversian canal. These spaces are empty

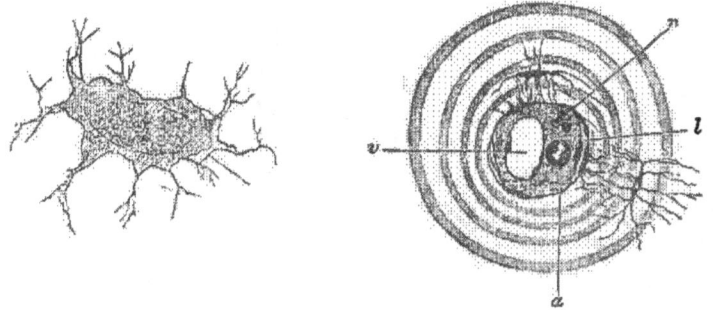

Fig. 15.—1, Bone Cell, highly magnified. 2, Haversian Canal and contents.

a, Arterial, v, Venous Capillary, n, Nerve. l, Lymphatics. Two Bone Corpuscles are shown communicating by Canaliculi with the Lymphatics: also several concentric Lamellæ.

in the dead, dried and ground-down bone, or at most filled with black detritus of bone and grindstone. The old histologists thought them to be empty during life, and called them *Lacunæ* or lakes; whilst the intercommunicating branches they called *Canaliculi*. We know now that the lacuna is simply the empty cavity which the bone cell occupies during life; whilst the canaliculi are filled by processes of the bone cells, by means of which nutrition is carried on.

Each Haversian canal is about $\frac{1}{500}$ of an inch in diameter. It contains, besides the above mentioned

THE CONNECTIVE SUBSTANCES. 37

vascular and nervous structures, a framework of white fibrous connective tissue and marrow.

The *intercellular substance* of bone is composed of white fibrous connective tissue with calcified interstices. It yields gelatine on boiling, and forms the basis of glue. The cement between the fibrils of the connective-tissue basement substance is filled with a deposit of lime salts, chiefly phosphates and carbonates. It is arranged in concentric circles around the Haversian canals, each circle being separated from its neighbor by a chain of lacunæ and canaliculi. Each concentric circle is called a *Lamella*.

Each Haversian canal with its contents, and with its concentric lamellæ and rings of bone cells and canaliculi forms an *Haversian System*. The entire compact bone is formed of closely aggregated Haversian systems. In cancellous bone the cells and intercellular substance are not so regularly arranged; the bone corpuscles are scattered at random in the calcified matrix.

The mineral matter in the intercellular substance of bone is in so finely divided a state that it is not visible to the highest powers of our microscope. Its presence can only be demonstrated by chemical means.

Bone is nourished in two ways; from the marrow inside it and from the periostium covering it. The nutrient artery of the bone penetrates its substance at the nutrient canal, reaches the marrow, subdivides and ramifies through it, and supplies the inner layers of the tissue. The periostium on the other hand sends down innumerable vessels which nourish the outer layers of the bone in contact with it.

The *Periostium* is a membrane composed of white fibrous connective tissue with a few elastic fibres. It closely covers the bone everywhere except at articular surfaces, or where bones are joined by ligament or cartilage. It carries the vessels and nerves not only for its own nutrition but also as above stated for that of the subjacent bone. Hence an inflammation and swelling of the periostium tears the vessels supplying, and this cuts off the nutrition from a plate of bone of a certain thickness lying under it ; and thus is explained the fact that periostitis always causes necrosis and exfoliation of bone.

The *Marrow* is found in the central cavities of long bones and in the cells and chambers of spongy bones. It consists of a fibrous connective-tissue network sustaining vessels and nerves. It contains a multitude of marrow cells, large spheroidal or irregular nucleated bodies; together with many fat cells and some larger multi-nucleated structures known as giant cells. Two varieties of marrow are found in the body. The yellow is the ordinary marrow of most adult mammals, and its color is due to the number of fat cells it contains. Red marrow is the ordinary marrow of the embryo ; it persists in the adult vertebræ, and is the only kind present in certain animals, such as the guinea pig and rabbit.

Development of Bone. Like the other connective substances bone is first laid down in mucoid tissue ; but this mucoid tissue soon develops in the embryo into cartilage or into a membrane. We therefore have two modes of development of bone :

1st, Ossification in cartilage. The cells of the hyaline cartilage gradually become arranged longitudinally ; blood-vessels penetrate the developing bone ; and lime salts are deposited in the intercellular substance. At the time of birth many of the bones or large portions of them are still in a state of cartilage. Thus are developed the long bones of the limbs, those of the vertebral column, the sternum and ribs, and the bones of the base of the skull.

2d, Ossification in membrane. Here only the infiltration of earthy salts occurs, and the cartilage cells become bone cells. In this way the bones of the face and the flat bones of the skull are formed.

In the teeth we find three varieties of bone which differ greatly from the ordinary kinds. Thus: the dentine is nearest to ordinary bone; the cement less so; and the enamel does not resemble the tissue it is derived from at all. These will be considered more in detail when studying the teeth.

CHAPTER VII.

The Muscular Tissue.

MUSCULAR Tissue is that tissue whose especial function is the production of motion. It is the eminently contractile tissue. It may be under the control of the will, as is the case with the ordinary muscles of dissection; or it may be entirely beyond our voluntary control, as are the muscular tissues of the internal organs. The two forms differ in their physical appearance, and hence are known as Striped or Striated Muscle and Unstriped or Smooth Muscle. The voluntary muscle is the striped or striated muscle, whilst the involuntary muscle is the unstriped or non-striated or smooth muscle. Cardiac Muscle, as we shall shortly see, combines some of the properties of both kinds, together with some special ones of its own thus forming a third variety.

Unstriped Muscle.

Unstriped muscle is the muscle of organic life, the muscle of the internal organs. It is present in large

THE MUSCULAR TISSUE. 41

amount in the body, though it is not so noticeable as the ordinary superficial muscles. It forms one of the coats and most of the mass of the intestinal canal, and a large part of the vascular system ; it is found in the skin, the bladder and the genito-urinary tract, and it forms almost the entire mass of the uterus, the prostate

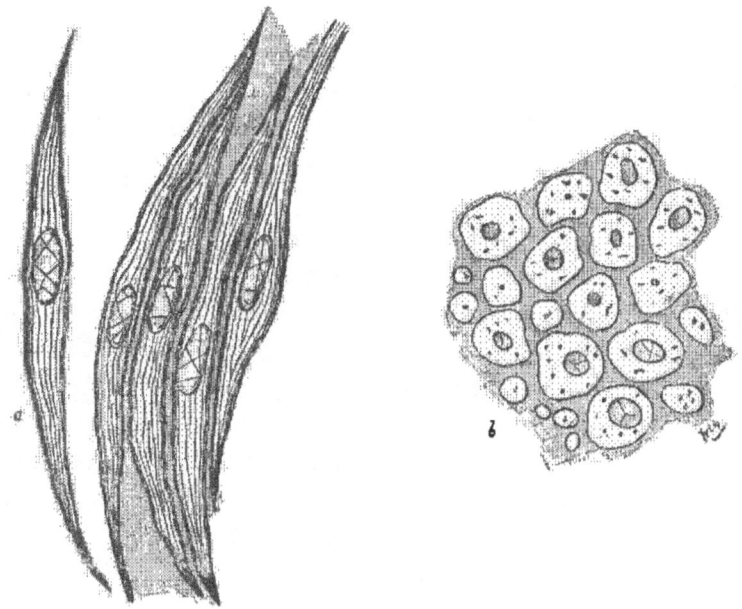

FIG. 16.—Unstriped Muscle.

a, Muscular Fibres with Interstitial Substance. *b*, Cross section of bundles of Fibres.

gland, etc. It consists of very long, nucleated, spindle-shaped cells, each one of which is called a contractile fibre. The contraction is longitudinal, the cells becoming shorter and thicker during the act. They vary from $\frac{1}{10}$ to $\frac{1}{500}$ of an inch in length. The nuclei are oval and often contain one or two nucleoli. A minute longitudinal striation is visible in the cell substance.

The intercellular substance is simply a small amount of albuminous cement that unites the cells together. Then the groups of cells are gathered into bundles by connective-tissue enclosures, in which partitions the vessels and nerves of the muscle run. The bundles thus formed vary greatly in size; in the blood-vessels, for instance, they are very minute, and run both around and parallel to the vessels, whilst in the bladder they form large meshes, and are visible to the naked eye.

Striated Muscle.

Striped muscle is composed of cylindrical fibres, some $\frac{1}{500}$ of an inch in diameter, and often more than one inch in length. The *Endomysium*, a delicate mmebrane of white fibrous connective tissue, unites the fibres into small bundles; and the *Perimysium*, a similar structure, unites these bundles into larger masses, forming the fasciculi that are visible to the naked eye. In this connective tissue run the vessels and nerves.

Each muscular fibre is enclosed in a delicate, transparent, elastic sheath called the *Sarcolemma*; it is visible only where the fibre has been partly torn, as a delicate thread uniting the separate ends. The substance of the fibre itself shows a distinct transverse marking of alternate dark and light stripes; whence arises the name of the tissue. The dark lines are membraneous partitions running across the fibre and attached to the sarcolemma. They are known as the *Partitions of Krause*, and with the sarcolemma form the membraneous framework that supports the contractile substance, which lies in the compartments thus formed.

The contractile substance itself is arranged into minute prismatic or rod-shaped elements which, placed side by side, fill up the compartments. They are known as the *Sarcous Elements of Bowman*, and

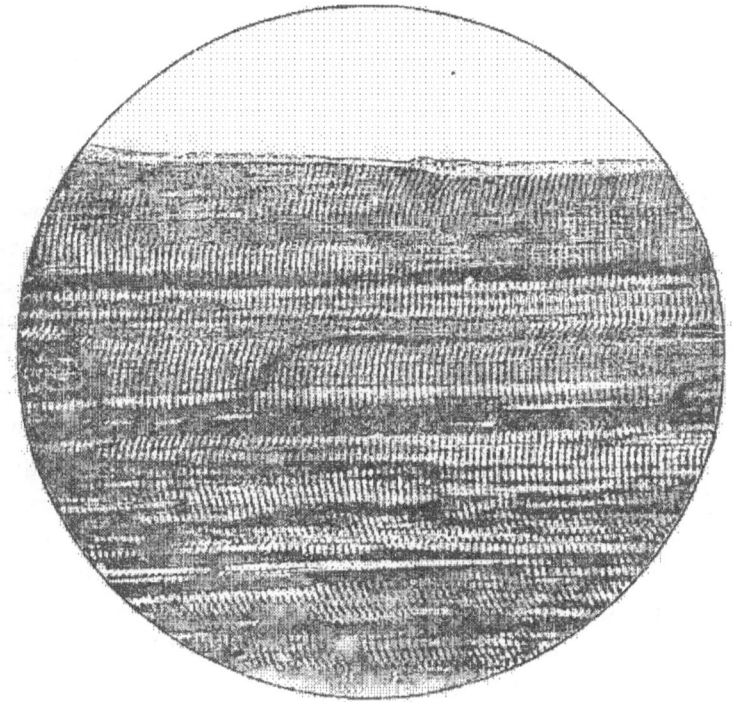

FIG. 17.—Striped Muscle.
Photograph magnified 500 times. (U. S. Army Medical Museum.)

though very close together, are not in actual juxtaposition; a minute layer of transparent interstitial substance, identical with the substance forming Krause's partitions, separates them. This partition between the individual sarcous elements becomes more marked after death and shrinkage, and leads to an appearance of longitudinal striation in the muscular fibre. Under certain circumstances the muscular fibre may then be split up into fibrillæ along the lines of these partitions between Bowman's elements; each fibril then consisting of a number of superimposed sarcous elements with fragments of Krause's membrane uniting them. The nuclei of the muscle fibres are known as *Muscle Corpuscles*. They are small oval bodies situated on the surface of the fibre, but within the sarcolemma. In the adult fibre there are but few of them; but they are numerous and large in young and rapidly growing ones. There are usually several to a single fibre.

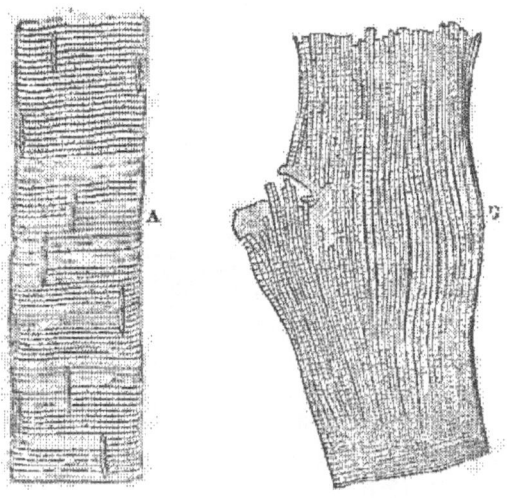

FIG. 18.—Voluntary Muscular Fibres.
a, Transverse Striation and Muscle Corpuscles.
b, Longitudinal Striæ and Fibrillæ.

Muscle fibre generally ends in tendon by the minute tendon bundles uniting directly with the sarcolemma of the fibre.

The vessels of striated muscle form a network in the perimysium and the endomysium. The nerves penetrate the sarcolemma and terminate in a ramified expansion known as an *End-plate*.

Cardiac Muscle.

The muscle of the heart is constructed on the same general plan as the striped muscle just considered, but shows some important histological differences there-

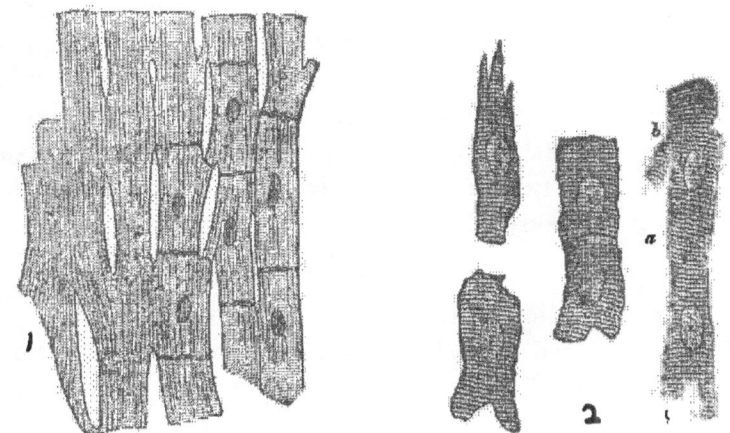

FIG. 19—Cardiac Muscle.

1. Magnified Cardiac Fibres, showing cross striæ, divisions, and junctions. (Schweigger-Seidel.) 2. Isolated Fibre Cells. *a*, Line of junction between two Cells. *b*, *c*, Branching Cells. (Neale.)

from besides the physiological one already noticed of not being under volitional control. These differences are :

1st, Cardiac muscle fibres possess no sarcolemma.

2d, The muscle corpuscles are in the centre of the fibres, not on their surface, and are more numerous than in ordinary striped muscle.

3d, Cardiac muscle fibres are distinctly divided into cell-like areas by partitions, and there is one muscle corpuscle to each area.

4th, Cardiac muscle fibres are branched, forming a close network.

CHAPTER VIII.

THE NERVOUS TISSUE.

THE Nervous Tissue consists of Nerve Cells of varying shape, and of Nerve Fibres of two distinct kinds, the whole being bound together by fibrous connective tissue. In the brain, spinal cord, and the sympathetic ganglia both cells and fibres are found; but the nerves, properly so-called, consist of fibres alone. The nervous is the irritable and automatic tissue of the body.

Nerve Fibres.

Two varieties of nerve fibres are found in the body, the Medullated or White, and the Non-medullated or Gray Fibres. The ordinary cerebro-spinal nerves are composed of the former, and the sympathetic nerves chiefly of the latter variety.

Medullated nerve fibres are double contoured, smooth, cylindrical fibres from $\frac{1}{800}$ to $\frac{1}{12000}$ of an inch in diameter. They consist of:

1st, The *Axis Cylinder*, a soft transparent thread which is continuous from end to end of the nerve.

THE NERVOUS TISSUE. 47

This is the essential conducting part of the nerve, and it exhibits a very delicate longitudinal striation, as if composed of still smaller fibrillæ.

2d, The *Medullary Sheath*, or *White Substance of Schwann*. This is the non-conducting envelope that

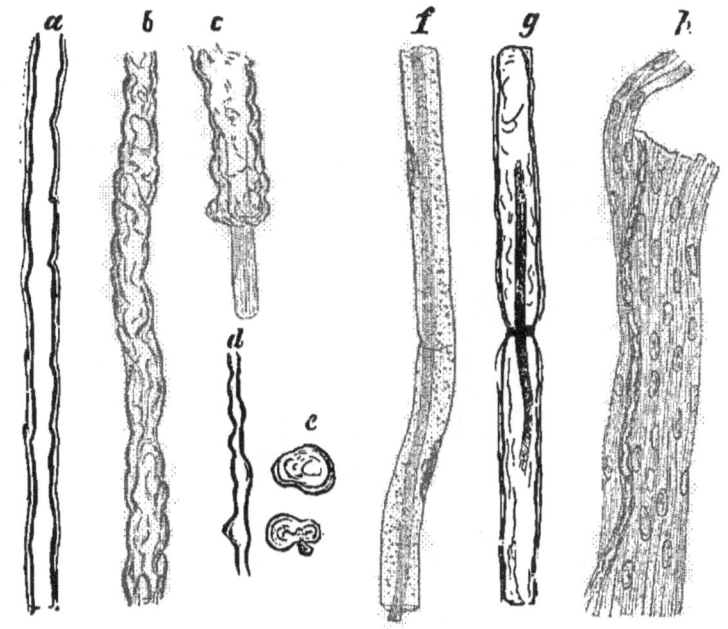

FIG. 20.—Nerve Fibres.

a, b, Medullated Nerve Fibres, untreated. *c, d,* Fibres of the Spinal Cord. *e,* Myeline Drops. *f,* Fibre showing the Axis Cylinder and Nerve Corpuscles. *g,* Fibre showing Ranvier's Crosses, and the divisions of the Neurilemma. *h,* Sympathetic Nerve Fibres with many Corpuscles; one Medullated Fibre is present.

protects the axis cylinder. It is a white, fatty, glistening substance called myelin, of considerable thickness, and gives to the nerve its white and shining appearance. Compressed out of the nerve, it forms fat-like masses.

3d, The *Neurilemma*, or *Sheath of Schwann* is the external envelope of the nerve fibre. It is a delicate, structureless membrane, which binds together and sustains the other semi-fluid contents of the fibre.

At certain regular intervals in the course of the nerve there appear constrictions due to an interruption

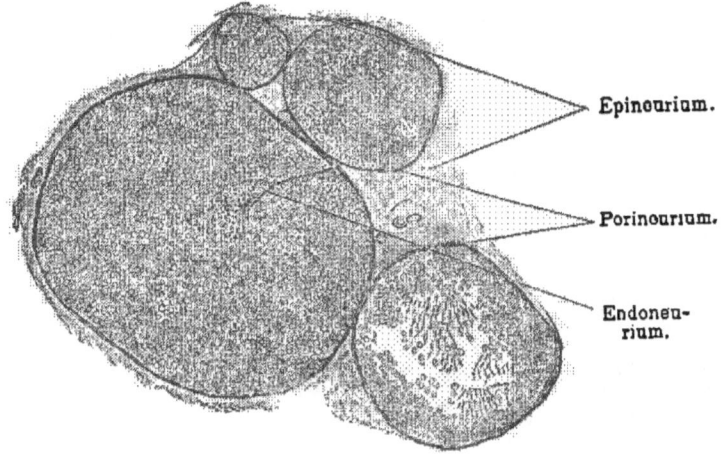

FIG. 21.—Nerve Fibres.
Cross section of Peripheral Spinal Nerve, enlarged 50 times. (Stohr.)

of the outer coats of the nerve, the neurilemma and the medulla. They are known as the *Nodes* or *Constrictions of Ranvier*. The portion of fibre between two nodes is known as an *Internodal Segment*. Each segment contains one of the third constituents of the nerve fibres.

3d, The *nerve corpuscles*. These are analogous to the muscle corpuscles, and lie upon the surface of the medullary sheath, just beneath the neurilemma. They consist of a small mass of protoplasm, with an oval nucleus imbedded in it.

Non-medullated nerve fibres are much smaller in size than the white fibres, and differ from them in branching and in having no medullary sheath at all. They consist simply of the axis cylinder and the neurilemma, with here and there a nucleated nerve corpuscle between the two.

Their small size and the absence of the white and glistening sheath of Schwann, are their chief characteristics.

A number of fibres are always collected together into a bundle, and they are held together by a delicate fibrous connective tissue called the *Endoneurium*. Surrounding such a bundle is more connective tissue, known as the *Perineurium*. Their bundles are then united into still larger groups by a connective tissue envelope, the *Epineurium*. The entire structure, together with fat cells, vessels, and lymphatics is contained in a tough sheath of the same white fibrous tissue, forming the microscopic sheath of the nerve.

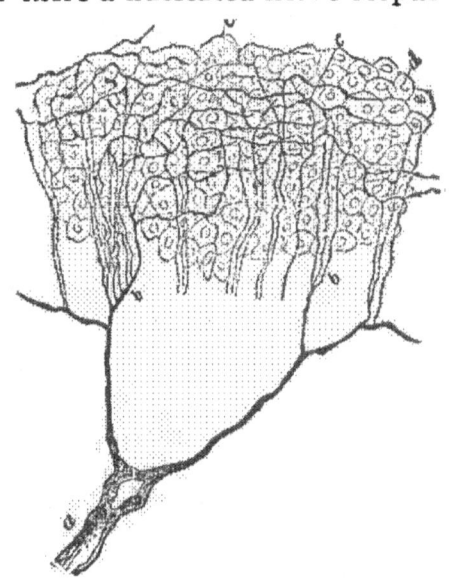

FIG. 22.—Fibrillar End Network of Nerve of Corneal Epithelium.

a, Axis Cylinder. *b*, Fibrillæ. *c*, Plexus among Corneal Cells. *d*, Epithelial Cells. (Handbook.)

In their terminations both central and peripheral nerves show many peculiarities of structure. As the nerve fibre approaches its central termination it loses first its medullary sheath, and presents the appearance of a gray or non-medullated fibre. It then loses its neurilemma, and proceeds a short distance as a naked axis cylinder. The neurilemma then becomes directly continuous with the axis cylinder process of a nerve cell.

The peripheral terminations are various and very complicated. The chief modes are as follows :

I. Terminations of Sensory Nerves—

1st, *In Networks of Fibrillæ.* The ordinary nerves of sensation of the skin and mucous membranes enter these organs, as above said, as naked axis cylinders. The axes then split up into their primitive fibrillæ, which form a network that ramifies among the epithelial cells, and terminates among them in free ends.

2d, *Pacinian Corpuscles*, found where the tactile sense is very acute, as in the palms and soles and in the genitals. They are oval, whitish bodies, sometimes $\frac{1}{20}$ of an inch in size, and visible to the naked eye. Each corpuscle is placed upon a stalk consisting of a single medullated nerve fibre, the neurilemma of which becomes continuous with the sheath of the pacinian body. The latter is composed of a number of concentric lamellæ of connective-tissue fibres embedded in a hyaline matrix, each lamella being lined with flattened endothelial cells. A narrow central space occupies the centre of the corpuscle ; and the nerve fibre pierces the various layers of the capsule to reach it. Here, in the central core, the naked axis cylinder ends in a plexus or a bulbous enlargement.

3d, *Tactile Corpuscles.* These are chiefly found in the palmar and plantar skin, and give to these parts their exquisite sensibility. They are much smaller than the Pacinian bodies, being only $\frac{1}{300}$ of an inch long on the average. Each one is an oval mass of connective tissue, into which enters a single medullated nerve

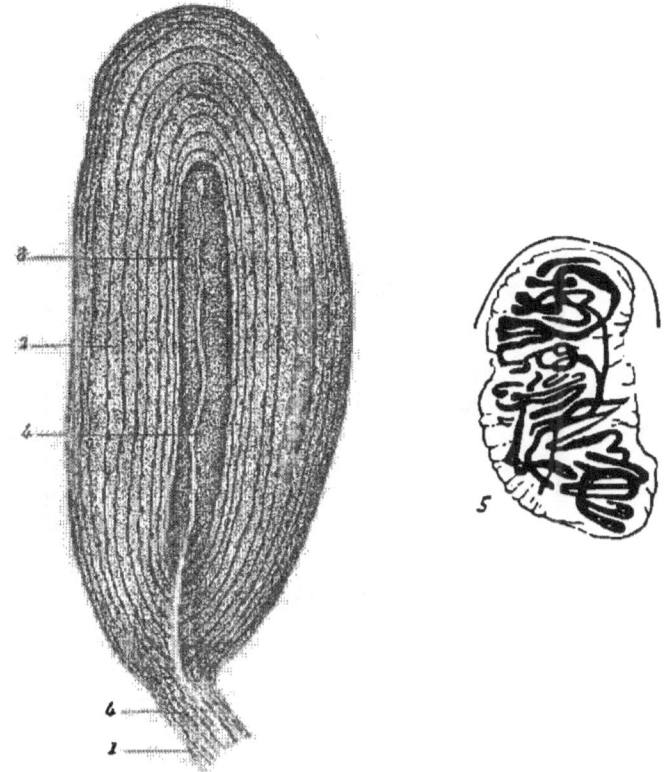

FIG. 23.—Pacinian Corpuscle and Tactile Corpuscle.

1, Stem of Pacinian Corpuscle. 2, Capsule. 3, Inner Capsule. 4, Axis Cylinder. 5. Tactile Corpuscle of Meissner.

fibre. The neurilemma becomes fused with the body of the corpuscle, the medullary sheath disappears, and the axis cylinder, after branching and anastomosing, terminates in bulbous enlargements.

52   A MANUAL OF GENERAL HISTOLOGY.

4th, *End Bulbs*, are similar to the tactile corpuscles. They are found in the conjunctiva and the male and female genital organs. The axis cylinder, after pursuing a convoluted course in the bulb, ends in the tuberous enlargements.

II. Terminations of Motor Nerves—

1st, *In Plexuses*. The non-medullated nerves from the sympathetic run in the connective tissue between

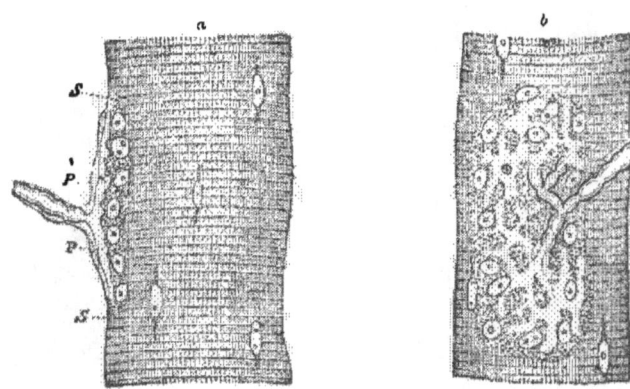

FIG. 24.—Termination of Motor Nerve.
a, End-plate seen edgewise; *b*, seen from the surface.

the bundles of smooth muscular fibres and, after dividing up into fibrillæ and forming plexuses, join the nuclei of the muscle cells.

2d, *In End-plates*. A medullated nerve fibre enters a voluntary muscular fibre at a right angle. The neurilemma becomes fused with the sarcolemma; the medullary sheath disappears; and the axis cylinder, after dividing up into fibrillæ, ends in a more or less granular plate which lies on the surface of the muscle fibre.

THE NERVOUS TISSUE.

Nerve Cells.

Nerve cells are found only in the gray matter of the nerve centres and in the various ganglia scattered

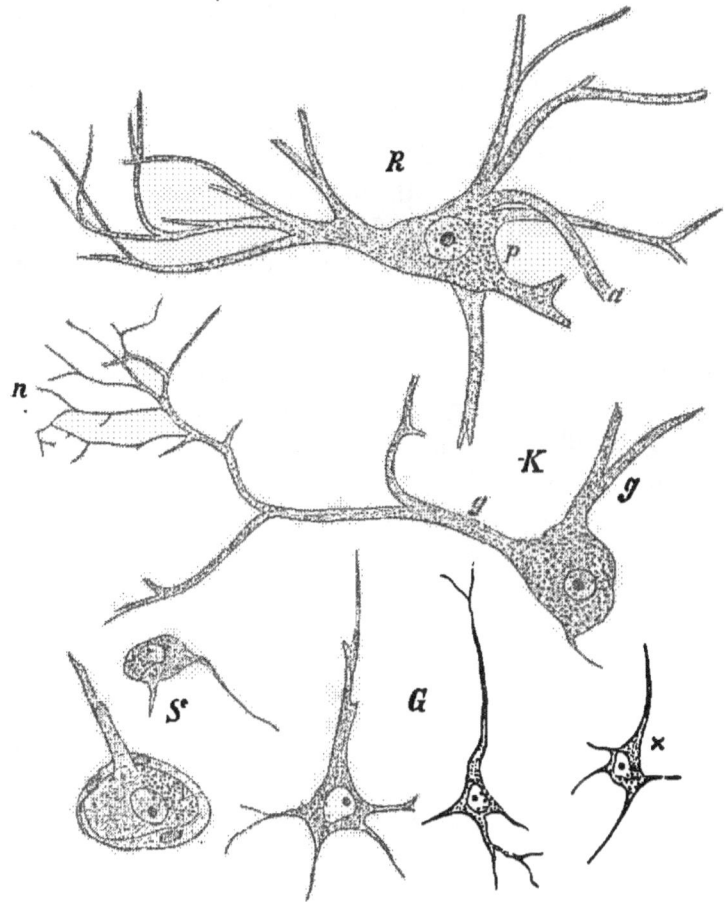

FIG. 25.—Nerve or Ganglion Cells.

n, Pigmented Multipolar Cell: *p*, Pigment; *a*, Axis Cylinder Process. K, Bipolar Cell; *g, g*, Processes; *n*, Plexus. G, Nerve Cells. s, *x*, Vater's and Spindle Cells.

throughout the body. They vary much in shape, being round, oval, or branched; they may have one or two, or a great number of processes. Some of them are amongst the largest cells found in the body, whilst others are very small indeed. The nucleus is usually large and spherical and contains a prominent nucleolus.

In accordance with the number of processes that it possesses, a nerve cell is called a *unipolar*, a *bipolar*, or a *multipolar cell*. One of these processes, at least, becomes continuous with the nerve fibre; whilst the others break up into a fine network that envelopes neighboring nerve cells and communicates with their processes.

In the nerve centres the cells and fibres are supported by a peculiar kind of connective tissue called *Neuroglia*. The granular interstitial substance is slightly fibrillated, and the cells are small, nucleated, and multi-branched.

PART II.

THE COMPOUND TISSUES.

The Compound Tissues are combinations of the Simple Tissues. They are bound together in various ways to form structures of more or less complexity.

CHAPTER IX.

THE VESSELS.

THESE are the tubes in which the blood and the lymph circulate. They form with the cavity of the heart a closed circuit which is everywhere lined with a continuous layer of endothelial cells.

The Bloodvessels.

Three different kinds are found in the body: Capillaries, Arteries and Veins.

Capillaries are the most abundant and the smallest, averaging $\frac{1}{3000}$ of an inch in diameter. They are simple tubes composed of a single layer of transparent endothelial cells. Each cell possesses an oval nucleus, and is bound by the next cells by a small amount of cement. In this cement there exist minute holes called *Stomata*, through which occurs the passage of the cellular elements of the blood when the vessel is distended in inflammation. The capillary is simply a vessel composed of the intima or general endothelial lining of the vascular system alone.

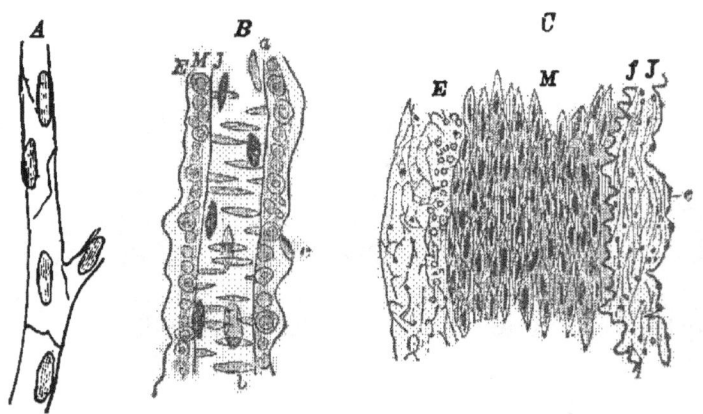

FIG. 26.—Vessels.

A, Capillary. B, Small Artery from Brain; J, Intima; M, Media; E, Adventitia; a, Nuclei of Endothelium of Intima; b, Nuclei of Muscle Cells of Media; c, Nuclei of Connective-tissue Cells of Adventitia. C, Transverse section of coat of large Artery; J, Intima; e, Nuclei of Endothelium; f, Fenestrated Membrane; M, Muscularis; E, Adventitia.

Arteries possess three coats, in accord with their greater size, strength and elasticity.

1st, The *Intima*, composed of endothelial cells as above stated, but with a substratum of elastic fibres.

2d, The *Media*, forming the chief mass of the walls of the vessel. It consists of elastic fibres and unstriped muscle in varying proportion. The larger arteries possess most elastic fibres; the smaller ones most muscular fibres. Thus the media of the aorta is composed almost entirely of yellow elastic fibres; whilst in the microscopic arteries it is composed of muscular tissue alone. The contractile fibres are arranged circularly around the vessel.

3d. The *Adventitia*, the external coat, composed of white fibrous connective tissue. Its thickness varies much, for on it depends the strength of the vessel. Its outer limit is indefinite, being merged with the fibrous sheath of the vessel.

The *Veins* are similar to the arteries in construction, but all their walls are thinner. Intima, media, and adventitia are weaker and of more delicate struc-

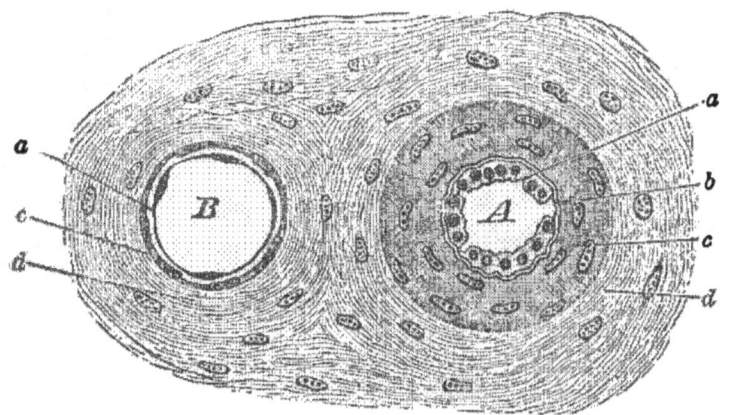

FIG. 27.—Cross section of Artery and Vein.

A, Artery; *a*, Intima with endothelial lining; *b*, Inner elastic coat; *c*, Media; *d*, Adventitia. B, Vein, same. (Wendt.)

ture, in accordance with their increased area for the blood and the lesser strain on their walls. They are peculiar also in possessing valves that hinder the reflux of the blood.

Large and medium sized arteries have bloodvessels of their own called Vasa Vasorum ; they also possess lymphatics.

The Lymph Vessels.

The large lymph vessels resemble the veins in structure ; but their walls are thinner and their valves more numerous. The lymphatic capillaries are much larger than the blood capillaries, but like them are tubes composed of a single layer of endothelial cells. They pervade the connective tissue of the various organs, commencing as clefts between the cells ; and the nutrient material flows from the blood capillary through the cells into the lymphatic vessel.

In the course of these vessels are many expansions lined with the same endothelium as the lymph vessels ; they are known as *Lymph Sinuses*, and are found in all the connective tissues. The *Synovial Cavities*, the *Cavity of the Tunica Vaginalis*, the *Subarachnoid Space*, the *Pleura*, the *Pericardium*, the *Peritoneum*, are all lymph sinuses and vast extensions of the lymphatic channels, and are in direct communication with the lymphatic system.

The glands connected with the lymphatic system will receive separate consideration later.

CHAPTER X.

MEMBRANES.

Mucous Membranes.

MUCOUS Membrane lines the internal cavities and passages of the body that communicate with the external air, as well as the various recesses, sinuses, and gland ducts that open into them. Being constantly exposed to external injury it is protected by the layer of thick, tenacious fluid, the mucous, that covers it. It is found in the gastro-pneumonic tract, lining the air passages, in the alimentary canal, the eyeball, and the ear; and in the genito-urinary tract, lining the urinary passages from the kidney down, as well as the genital passages, both male and female.

Mucous membrane consists of three layers:

1st, An *Epithelial Layer* covering the surface; it may be scaly or stratified, as in the mouth or throat, or columnar as in the intestines, or ciliated as in parts of the respiratory tract and in the uterus.

2d, The *Corium*, below the epithelium. This is composed of white fibrous and elastic tissue mixed, and sustains the bloodvessels and nerves of the tissue.

60 A MANUAL OF GENERAL HISTOLOGY.

3d, The *Muscularis Mucosæ*, an irregular layer of unstriped muscular fibres. The bloodvessels of the mucous membranes are abundant, as also are the lymphatics; the nervous supply varies much in different locations. The surface of the membrane is some-

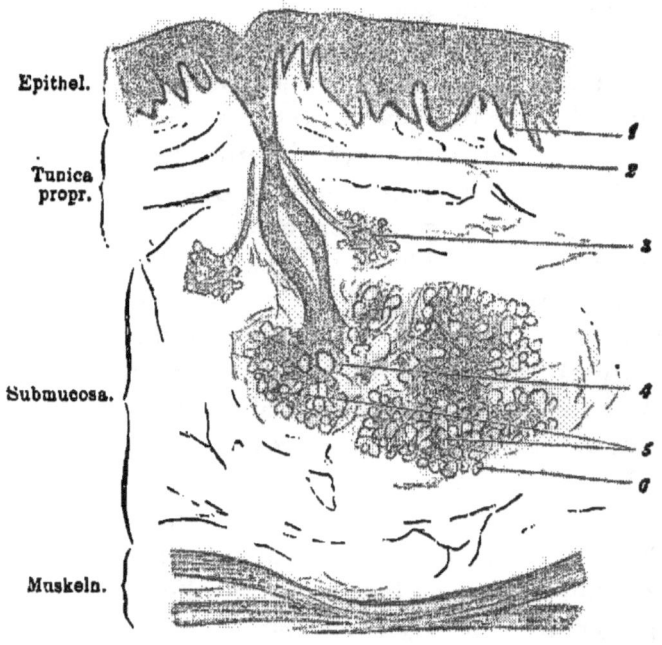

Fig. 28.—Transverse section of Mucous Membrane of the Lips.

1, Papillæ. 2, Excretory Canal of Gland. 3, 5, Mucous Glands. 4, 6, Transverse section of an Excretory Duct.

times smooth and sometimes covered with *Papillæ* or *Villi*. The papillæ are papular elevations such as are found on the tongue; they contain vessels and nerves, and serve either as mere extensions of the membrane or contain the organs of taste or touch. The villi are found in the small intestine. They are small elevations containing vessels and lacteals.

Most glands pour their secretion onto surfaces covered with mucous membrane, but the *Mucous Glands* are a part of its structure and elaborate the mucous. They are tubular recesses of the basement membrane lined with the epithelial coat. They abound especially in the gastro-intestinal and uterine mucous membranes.

Mucous itself is a viscid fluid containing mucin. It is produced by the epithelial cells lining the tubular glands; they swell up with it, burst, and pour out their contents upon the membrane.

Serous Membranes.

The serous membranes line those cavities of the body that have no outlet, the pleuræ, peritoneum, pericardium, arachnoid and subarachnoid spaces, and the tunica vaginalis. They are thin, transparent membranes, consisting of:

1st, An *Endothelial Layer*, a single layer of flat, large, nucleated endothelial cells.

2d, A *Basement Layer* consisting of fibrous tissue and containing the vessels, nerves, and lymphatics.

The *Serum* is a thin coagulable fluid present only in sufficient quantity to lubricate the parts.

Synovial Membranes.

The synovial membranes are in structure very like the serous ones; they surround the cavities of the joints, and other parts that are mobile, as the bursæ, between tendons and the bones that they play over, and the synovial sheaths, which surround many of the tendons. They consist of:

1st, An *Endothelial Layer* of large, nucleated, endothelial cells.

2d, A *Basement Layer* of fibrous tissue containing the vessels and nerves. They all secrete *Synovia*, a viscid, glairy yellow fluid that lubricates their surfaces.

PART III.

THE ORGANS.

The Organs are built up by the combination of Compound and Simple Tissues, and are, therefore, frequently of extremely complex structure. Their description will complete our study of the structure of the animal body.

CHAPTER XI.

THE GLANDS.

Lymphatic Glands.

LYMPHATIC Glands are structures of varying size found in connection with the lymphatic vessels, and composed of a peculiar tissue known as *Lymphoid* or *Adenoid Tissue*. This consists of a network or reticulum of connective tissue, in the meshes of which are large numbers of round lymphoid cells. Collected into masses in various parts of the body there are found the structures known as *Lymphatic Glands;* but the name is incorrect, since they are not glands and have no secretion. They are better called *Lymphatic Nodes*. They occur as Simple and Compound Lymphatic Nodes.

Simple Lymphatic Nodes or Lymph Follicles are found in the upper part of the pharynx (pharyngeal tonsil), in the small and large intestine (solitary

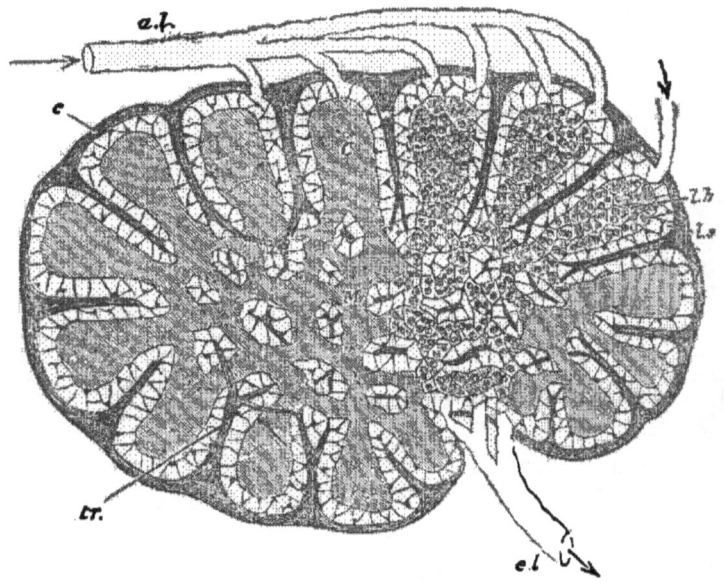

FIG. 29.—Lymphatic Gland in diagrammatic section.
a, b, Afferent Lymphatics. e, l, Efferent Lymphatics. c, Cortex. M, Reticulated Cords of Medullary Substance. l, s, Lymph Sinus. c, Fibrous Coat with Trabeculæ, tr.

glands), in the ileum as the agminated glands or Peyer's patches, and in the thymus and spleen. They consist of:

1st, An adenoid reticulum, a network of fibrils which forms the framework of the follicle.

2d, Small, flat endothelial cells attached to the reticulum.

3d, A mass of lymph corpuscles or lymph cells which fills up the network. These are large round cells with one or more nuclei, showing marked amoeboid motion.

The *Tonsils* are masses of lymph follicles bound together by connective tissue. Their free surface is covered with mucous membrane, in which are a number of large involutions or crypts ; numerous mucous glands open into these depressions.

The *Pharyngeal Tonsil of Luschka* is situated in the upper pharynx, and is similar to the tonsils in structure.

The *Thymus Gland* is composed of lymphatic follicles in a dense connective-tissue framework, in which run lymphatic vessels, bloodvessels, etc.

Peyer's Patches are collections of simple lymphatic follicles.

The *Malpigian Corpuscles of the Spleen* are small masses of lymphoid tissue. Lymphoid tissue also occurs in other portions of the body in a more diffuse form. This is especially the case in various parts of the intestinal and respiratory mucous membrane.

Compound Lymphatic Nodes are found all over the body interpolated in the course of the lymphatic vessels. Thus we have the mesenteric, portal, bronchial, sternal, cervical, popliteal, inguinal, and lumbar nodes. Each gland is enveloped in a *Capsule* of white, fibrous connective tissue, from which *Septa* are sent off that divide the gland into a number of incomplete compartments. In these run the vessels and nerves. Sections of the gland show it to be composed of an outer or cortical and denser portion, and an inner or medullary part of softer consistency. This is

·due to the varying amount of connective tissue of the framework.

The interior of the gland is filled with adenoid tissue, a delicate reticulum containing a mass of lymphoid cells. Between the reticular masses and the trabeculæ are spaces through which the lymphatic fluid circulates, known as *Lymph Sinuses*, which are completely lined with endothelial cells. The *Afferent Lymph Vessels* enter the gland at the depression known as the *Hilum*, and open directly into these sinuses. The fluid circulates through the sinuses, and leaves the gland by the efferent vessel at the hilum. Hence, the lymphatic nodes may be regarded as filters interposed in the course of the lymphatic current.

Salivary Glands.

The salivary are the typical secreting glands. They are called racemose from their essential parts being arranged like grapes on a stalk. They are composed essentially of a mass of secreting epithelial cells, polyhedral or columnar in shape, and with large and prominent nuclei. In the process of secretion they become granular, swell up, burst and discharge their contents into the duct. They are of two kinds:

1st, *Mucous Cells*, large and granular, producing mucigen, and furnishing the mucoid secretion.

2d, *Albuminous Cells*, smaller in size and secreting the true serous saliva.

The various salivary glands contain these cells in varying proportion, and differ accordingly in the nature of their secretion. The Parotid in man and animals, the Submaxillary and Orbital in the rabbit, and the Submaxillary in the guinea pig contain the second kind almost exclusively, and secrete a true saliva. The Submaxillary and the Sublingual, on the other hand, in most animals contain chiefly the first kind of cell, and secrete a mucous fluid with but little ptyalin in it.

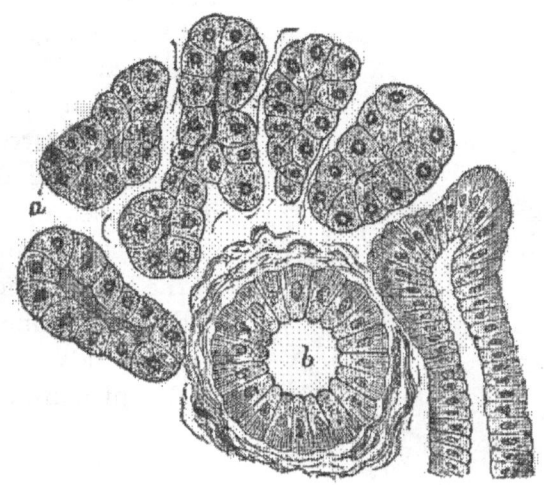

Fig. 30.—Section of Human Submaxillary Gland.
a, Gland Alveoli, lined with Salivary Cells. *b*, Interlobular Duct, cut transversely. (Atlas.)

The secreting cells are united into groups known as *Alveoli* or *Acini*, forming flask-shaped branches. A *Basement Membrane* of fibrous connective tissue encloses and sustains each alveolus. A number of acini are bound together by connective tissue to form *Lobules;* and an outer envelope of the same material forms the *Capsule* of the gland.

The *Vessels* are abundant and form a capillary network around the alveoli. The larger vessels ramify in the fibrous septa of the gland. The *Lymphatics* begin as lacunar vessels lying around the alveoli. The *Nerves* come both from the cerebro-spinal axis and the sympathetic, and connect directly with the cells of the alveoli.

The Pancreas.

The Pancreas is a compound racemose gland with a structure similar to that of the salivary glands just described. There is the same connective-tissue framework surrounding the gland and dividing it into lobes and lobules; the same arrangement of the vessels and ducts, and the same flask-shaped alveoli lined with epithelium.

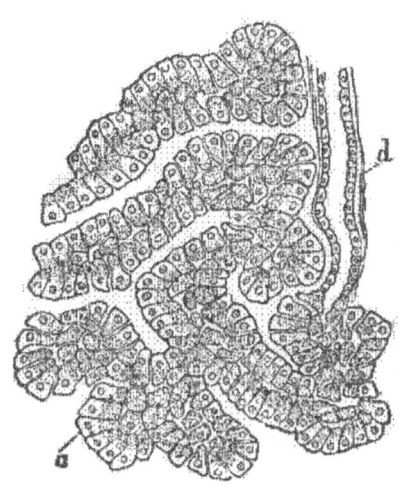

FIG. 81.—Pancreas of Dog.
a, Alveoli of Gland. *d*, Duct.

The Mammary Gland.

The Mammary Gland is a racemose gland composed of cuboidal epithelial cells arranged in alveoli. The alveoli are elongated or flask-shaped; each is lined by a layer of polyhedral or columnar epithelial cells resting on a membrane propria of connective tissue. Septa of connective tissue divide the alveoli from one another, and support them; and this connective tissue frequently contains a large amount of fat. The ducts into which the alveoli open are small, and are composed of a membrane propria lined with short columnar epithelial cells. The larger ducts are thicker, and have much unstriped muscular fibre in their walls. This unstriped muscle is continous with the involuntary muscle that is present in the skin of the nipple.

In the mammary gland of children and in that of the adult male and the non-pregnant and non-suckling female, the fibrous tissue is prominent and the alveoli are comparatively few. These latter are then solid

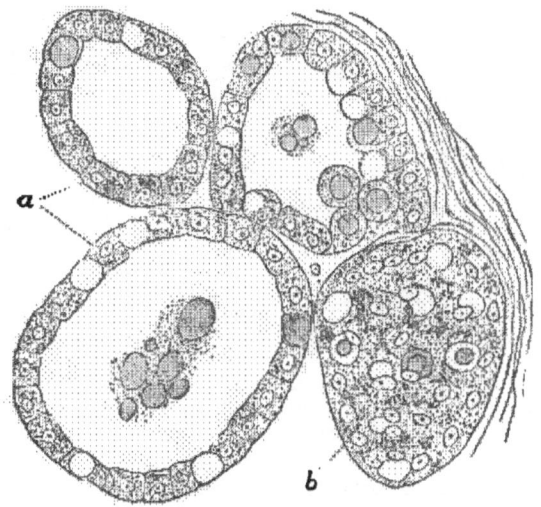

FIG. 32.—Mammary Gland of Cat in later stage of Pregnancy.

a, Epithelial Cells of Alveoli, some filling up with Fat. *b*, Same seen on surface; Milk Globules and Granular Matter in the Cavities.

cylinders, being filled up with polyhedral and granular epithelial cells. When pregnancy occurs the epithelial cells rapidly multiply; the alveoli enlarge and elongate. When the milk secretion begins the central mass of cells in the alveoli undergoes fatty degeneration and is cast off, forming the *Colostrum*.

In the active gland the cells lining the acini produce oil globules from their own substance. These globules coalesce, swell out the cell, cause its rupture, and are extruded as *Milk Globules*. Each such globule is covered with a delicate layer of albumen from the cell protoplasm. The epithelial cell itself returns to its normal condition after extrusion of the milk globule, and begins the process anew.

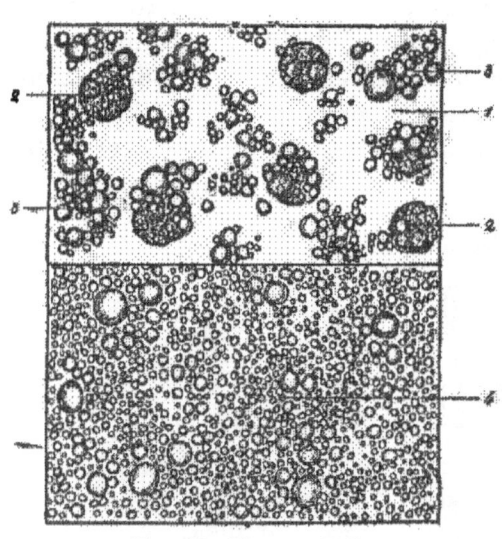

FIG. 33.—Human Milk.

1, First Day after Confinement. 2, Colustrum Corpuscles. 3, Free Fat Globules. 4, Milk at Sixteenth Day after Confinement.

The *Bloodvessels* of the alveoli are extremely numerous, especially during lactation. Lymph spaces and vessels are abundant in the inter-alveolar septa.

CHAPTER XII.

THE GLANDS. (*Continued.*)

The Spleen.

THE Spleen is, on the whole, somewhat similar in structure to the lymphatic glands, but differs from them in a number of important respects. Its parenchyma is composed of a reddish-brown mass called the *Pulp*, in which are imbedded a number of small grayish bodies, the *Malphigian Corpuscles*.

The *Pulp* is made up of a delicate network of septa known as the *Pulp Cords*. The meshes of this network are filled up with a mass of large spheroidal endothelial cells, with the remnants of broken down red blood cells, particles of blood pigment, etc. Into this mass open the radicles of the splenic artery, the vessels of the Malphigian tufts. In it also are the *Venous Sinuses*, oblong spaces lined with endothelial cells which open into the smallest veins. These venules run along the trabeculæ of the organ, and unite to form the splenic vein.

72 A MANUAL OF GENERAL HISTOLOGY.

The *Malphigian Corpuscles* lie imbedded in the splenic pulp. They are, in fact, lymphatic nodules; being composed of a net of adenoid tissue with the round lymphoid cells in its meshes. Each corpuscle is a grayish, globular body, attached, as it were, to the terminal filament of a splenic arteriole. The

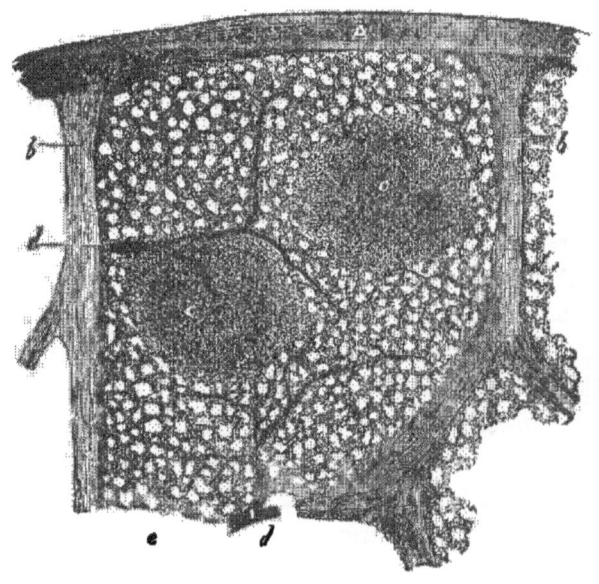

FIG. 34.—Spleen.

Vertical section of a small superficial portion of human Spleen, low amplification. A, Peritoneal and Fibrous Covering. *b*, Trabeculæ. *c*, *c*, Malphigian Corpuscles, in one of which an Artery is cut transversely. *d*, Injected Arterial Twig. *e*, Spleen Pulp. (Kölliker.)

adenoid tissue of the corpuscle and the coats of the arteriole become fused; and the blood, after leaving the tuft, percolates through the splenic pulp, and is collected again in the venous sinuses, and so attains the splenic vein. The red blood cells seem to be

THE GLANDS.

taken up by the endothelial cells of the pulp, for they can be seen inside them; they are then apparently broken up, leaving a granular detritus behind. In fact, the splenic pulp seems to destroy the red blood cells; whilst the white blood cells apparently originate there directly from the endothelial cells.

The entire spleen is enclosed in a *capsule* of connective tissue which contains also elastic fibres and a considerable quantity of unstriped muscle in its substance.

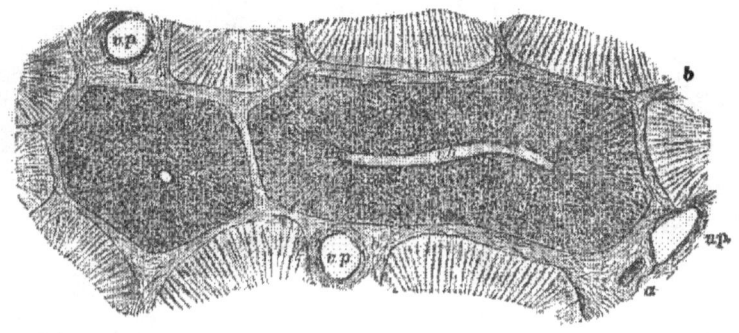

FIG. 35.—Section of Pig's Liver.

a, h, Hepatic Vein. *v, p,* Portal Vein. *a,* Hepatic Artery. *b,* Connective Tissue of Glisson's Capsule.

Externally this capsule is covered with a layer of endothelial cells, being a part of the general peritoneum. Trabeculæ go thence into the interior of the organ dividing it into a number of imperfect compartments. They unite at the hilum to form the mass of connective tissue that supports the vessels and nerves. Lymphatic plexuses are found in the adventitia of the larger arteries; and sympathetic nerve fibres accompany them.

The Liver.

The Liver is composed of polygonal epithelial cells, each about $\frac{1}{1000}$ of an inch in diameter. Their protoplasm is granular and distinctly reticulated; they have large spherical nuclei, and sometimes one or more nucleoli. Adjacent cells are united by an albuminous cement in very minute quantity; but narrow

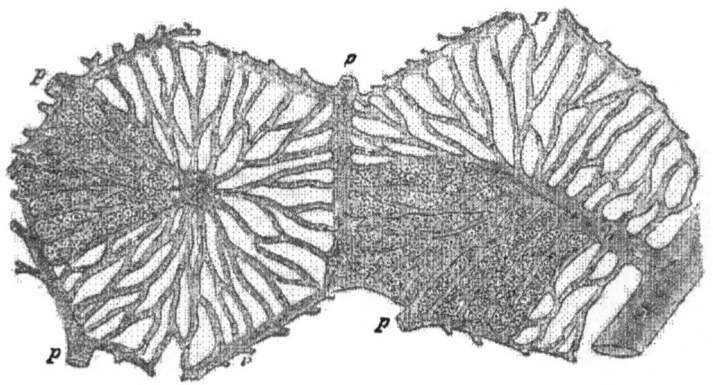

FIG. 36.—Diagrammatic representation of two Hepatic Lobules.

The left-hand Lobule is represented with the Intralobular Vein cut across; on the right-hand one the Section takes the course of the Intralobular Vein. *p*, Interlobular branches of the Portal Vein. *h*, Intralobular branches of the Hepatic Vein. *s*, Sublobular Vein. *c*, Capillaries of Lobules. The arrows indicate the course of the Blood. The Liver Cells are only represented in a part of each Lobule. (Schaefer.)

passages are left between the cells, forming the beginnings of bile capillaries and carrying off the secretion of the organ.

The *Liver Cells* are aggregated into groups called *Lobules* or *Acini*, $\frac{1}{20}$ of an inch in size. Each acinus is surrounded by a framework of white fibrous connective tissue which sends delicate tendrils through the lobule, supporting the cells that compose it. This

THE GLANDS. 75

framework is much thicker and stronger in some animals, as the pig, than it is in man and the carnivora. It supports the vascular, lymphatic nervous, and biliary structures of the liver.

In the centre of each lobule, unsupported by connective tissue, lies the beginning of the *Hepatic Vein*. The capillaries running between the hepatic cells converge towards it and unite there. At the periphery of the lobule, where two or more lobules join, there is a

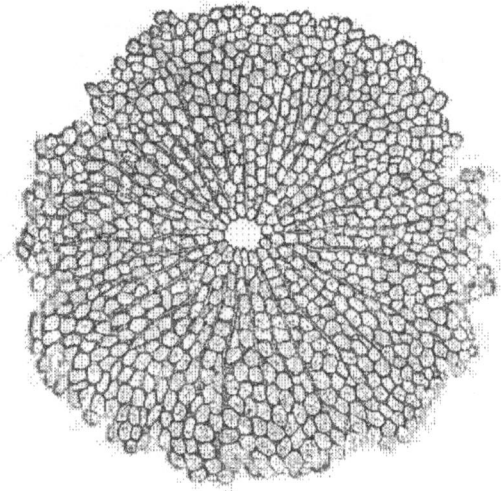

FIG. 37.—Transverse section of Human Lobule, showing opening of Hepatic Vein. (Eckert.)

mass of connective tissue, a thickening of the capsule, containing the *Portal Vein*, the *Hepatic Artery*, and the *Bile Ducts*. This mass of connective tissue surrounds and accompanies the vessels to the hilum, and is known as the *Capsule of Glisson*.

The entire organ is covered with a serous membrane consisting of a fibrous connective-tissue covered with endothelial cells. It is a part of the general peritoneal membrane. At the Hilum this fibrous coat is continued into the organ around the vessels; and

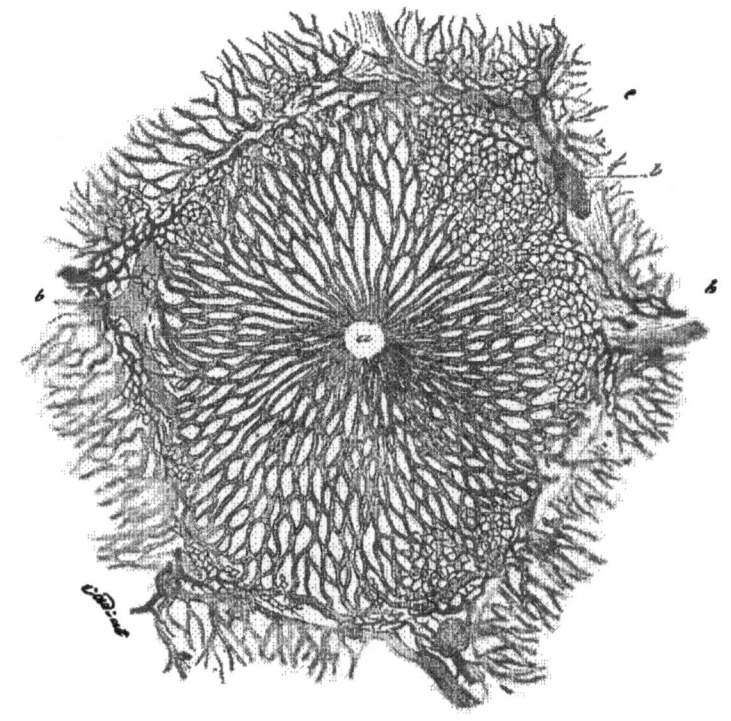

Fig. 38.—Lobule of Rabbit's Liver: Vessels and Bile Ducts injected; Liver Cells removed.

  a, Central or Hepatic Vein. b, Peripheral or Intralobular Veins. c, Bile Ducts. (Cadiat.)

there, as the capsule of Glisson, it forms the framework of the liver.

The *Portal Vein* enters the liver at the hilum, ramifies in the capsule of Glisson, breaks up into capillaries in the interlobular connective tissue, and

THE GLANDS.

forms plexuses around the acini. These are the *Interlobular Veins*, and from them capillaries radiate into the interior of the lobule with frequent anastomoses. In the centre of the acinus the capillaries become confluent as the *Intralobular (Hepatic) Vein*. The intralobular veins of neighboring acini flow into the *Sublobular Vein* that lies below them. The sublobular veins unite to form the larger hepatic veins, which pass out of the liver at the hilum.

The *Hepatic Artery* enters the organ at the hilum, ramifies in the areolar tissue of Glisson's capsule, and supplies it and the bile ducts. Its capillaries flow into the interlobular veins.

The *Bile Ducts* begin as simple channels between adjacent liver cells, and these run into *Interlobular Bile Ducts* which run in Glisson's capsule. They consist of a delicate membrana propria and a layer of polyhedral epithelial cells. They join into interlobular bile ducts which pass out at the hilum as the *Hepatic Duct*.

The *Lymphatics* form plexuses in the interlobular connective tissue ; and there also the nerves are found.

CHAPTER XIII.

THE ALIMENTARY CANAL.

THE Alimentary Canal in general is composed of three coats, an internal one of mucous membrane, a middle one of unstriped muscular fibres, and an external one of white fibrous connective tissue. In certain situations a fourth serous coat, formed by the peritoneum, is present.

The Teeth.

The *Teeth* are composed of three calcified tissues. The *Enamel* covering the crown or exposed portion is of epithelial origin; but the *Dentine*, forming the bulk of the tooth and enclosing the pulp cavity, and the *Cement* which covers the part of the tooth within the socket, are connective tissues. A *Periostium* of dense fibrous tissue similar to that of the bones covers the cement.

The *Enamel* is composed of elongated hexagonal prisms closely packed together and set vertically to the surface of the tooth. Transverse sections show a

THE ALIMENTARY CANAL. 79

minute amount of interstitial cement substance uniting the prisms. They are composed of lime and magnesium salts, chiefly phosphates and carbonates. In the young tooth a layer of epithelial cells covers the

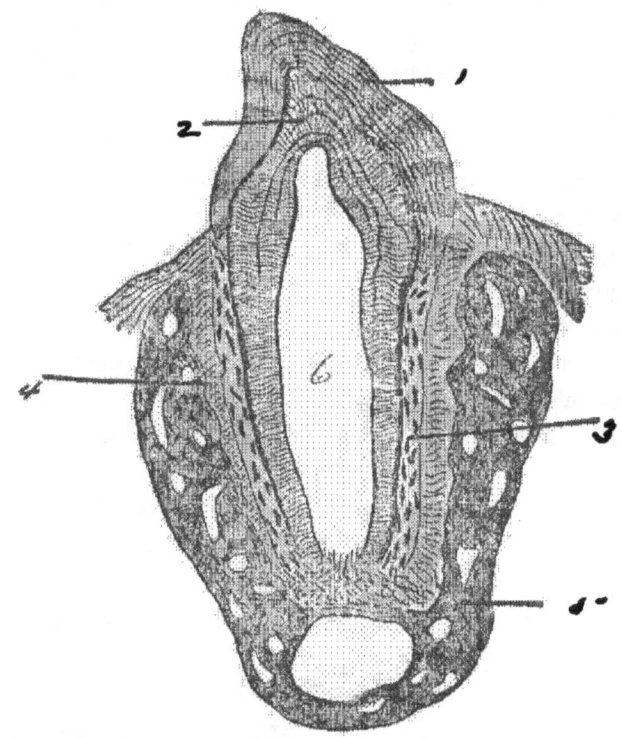

FIG. 39.—Longitudinal section of Incisor Tooth in situ.

1, Enamel. 2, Dentine. 3, Cement. 4, Dental Periostium. 5, Bone of Lower Jaw. 6, Pulp Cavity.

enamel, the *Cuticle of Nasmyth;* this "skin of the teeth" is, however, soon destroyed by use.

The *Dentine* forms the mass of the tooth, and encloses the pulp cavity. It is similar to bone in its structure, but contains neither Haversian canals nor lacunæ. It consists of a matrix of fine fibrillar connective tissue impregnated with lime salts like that of bone. In this are imbedded the *Dentinal Tubules*, parallel branching tubes which run from the pulp cavity to the cement and enamel outside. In the tubules are the *Dentinal Fibres*, protoplasmic prolongations of the superficial cells of the pulp, the Odontoblasts.

The *Cement* or *Crusta Petrosa* covers that part of the dentine which is within the socket in the jaw. It resembles true bone more than any other structure of the teeth, containing bone corpuscles and lamellæ, but no Haversian canals.

The *Pulp* fills up the central cavity in the dentine. It is composed of a loose mucoid connective-tissue framework which sustains a very abundant network of vessels. Medulated nerve fibres are also plentiful; the naked axis cylinders ascend into the dentinal tubules. The outer surface of the pulp is covered with a layer of large nucleated spindle cells, the *Odontoblasts*, whose outer processes enter the dentinal tubules and become a dentinal fibre. By them the dentine is formed.

The Mouth.

The *Mouth* is clothed with a mucous membrane composed of a fibrous framework with papillary elevations, and covered with a thick layer of stratified pavement epithelium. An abundance of vessels, nerves, and lymphatics, with some unstriped muscle, is present in the sub-epithelial layer. There are also serous and mucous glands lined with secreting epithelium of the ordinary type. *Tactile Corpuscles* are present in the papillæ of the lips.

The Tongue.

The *Tongue* is composed of striated muscular fibres covered with a papillated layer of thick stratified epithelium. On its lower surface the mucous membrane is similar to that of the rest of the buccal cavity; but

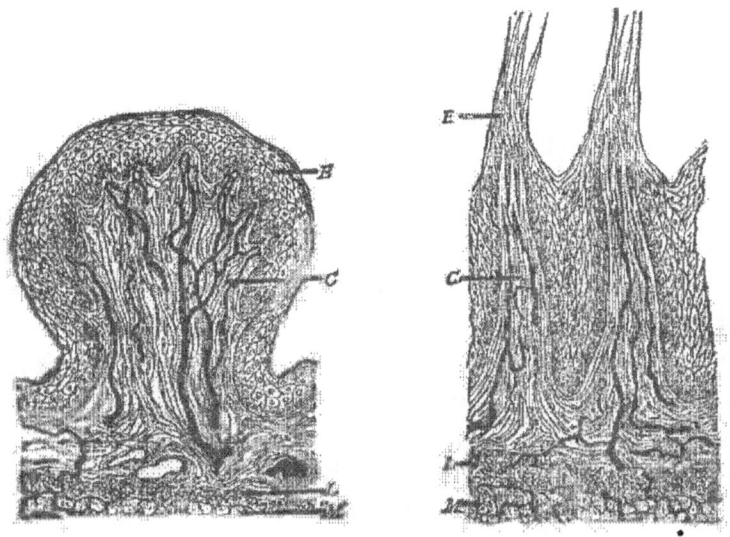

FIG. 40.—Tongue: Fungiform and Filiform Papillæ.
E, Epithelium. C, Corium. L, Lymphatics. M, Muscular Fibres.

on its upper surface it is thicker and is provided with certain special structures, Papillæ, Glands, and Taste-buds.

The *Papillæ* are of three kinds:

1st, *Filiform Papillæ*, conical elevations of the mucous membrane, covered with a cap of fringed epithelium. They are the most abundant of the papillary structures of the tongue and occupy the entire dorsum of the organ.

2d, *Fungiform Papillæ*, larger, mushroom-like structures, very vascular and partly imbedded in depressions of the mucous membrane. They are scattered here and there among the filiform papillæ, and are simple club-shaped elevations of the mucous membrane.

3d, *Circumvallate Papillæ*. There are twelve of these on the dorsum of the tongue, forming large conical projections surrounded by a groove and an external raised wall of the mucous membrane. They are arranged in a V-shaped line on the back of the tongue. They contain the taste-buds in the epithelium of their surface and receive filaments of the glossopharyngeal nerve.

The *Glands* are numerous. Most of them secrete mucous; but a few in the trenches of the circumvallate papillæ secrete a serous fluid. They are simple tubular glands lined with secreting epithelium.

The *Taste-buds* are mostly situated in the epithelium of the circumvallate and fungiform papillæ; a few are found elsewhere in the dorsal mucous membrane, and also in that of the soft palate and the epiglottis. They are barrel-shaped masses of cells placed vertically in the epithelium and resting on the fibrous tissue of the mucous membrane. They are composed of a mass of flattened epithelial cells which sustain the special taste or gustatory cells, and form a covering for the bud. The *Gustatory Cells* are elongated, bipolar, large nucleated cells; the outer pole ends in a delicate, cilium-like process which projects through a minute pore or opening on the surface epithelium; the inner pole is directly continuous with a nerve fibre in the mucosa.

The Œsophagus.

The Œsophagus possesses :

1st, An *Internal coat of Mucous Membrane*. Its fibrous layer is papillary, and the epithelium covering it is of the thick and stratified variety. Small mucous glands open on its surface. It contains also a quantity of irregularly arranged smooth muscular fibres, the *Muscularis Mucosæ*.

2d, The *Muscular Coat* lies outside the mucosa. Its upper third is of voluntary muscle, whilst the lower portion is of the involuntary variety. It is arranged in two layers, an inner longitudinal and an outer circular layer.

3d, The *External Coat* is formed of white fibrous connective tissue. The vessels are abundant, and ascend up into the papillæ; lymphatics and nerves are also plentiful.

CHAPTER XIV.

THE ALIMENTARY CANAL. (*Continued.*)

The Stomach.

THE Stomach posseses four coats: an internal mucous, an areolar coat of connective tissue, a muscular, and a serous coat.

The *Mucous Membrane* is thick and soft, and contains the important glandular structures of the organ. The connective tissue basement substance of the membrane is filled with the long tubular glands that secrete the gastric juice and the mucous. So closely are they set that their openings give to the surface of the mucosa a reticulated appearance; and sections appear plicated and villous. The surface epitheium is a thin layer of the columnar variety. Smooth muscular fibres are present in abundance, and form a *Muscularis Mucosæ* that can be divided into an outer circular and an inner longitudinal layer; and bundles of muscle cells pass up therefrom to the surface, forming longitudinal muscular sheaths around the ducts of the glands. The vessels form a dense plexus around the glandular structures; lymphatics and nerves do the same.

The *glandular structures of the mucosa* are of two distinct kinds:

1st, The *Peptic Glands*. These are wavy tubes extending through the mucous membrane. Two or three join together to open into a single short duct, which is lined with columnar epithelium like that of the surface. The glands themselves have a basement membrane, lined with a layer of transparent granular epithelial cells

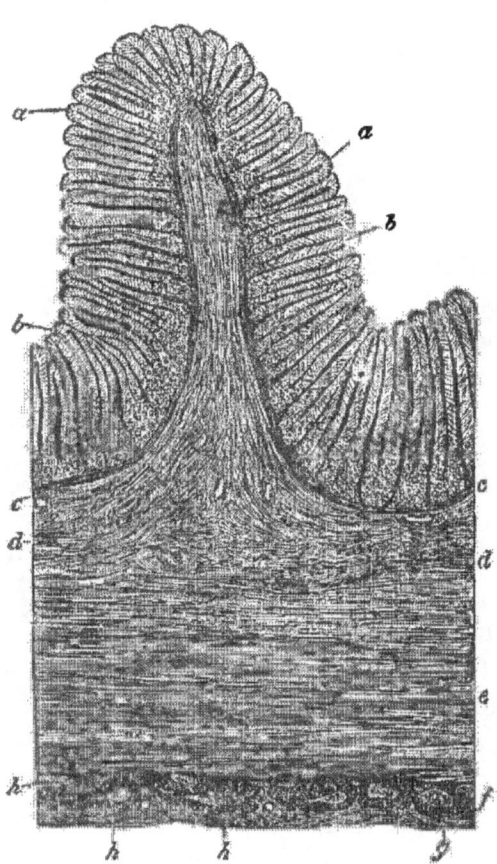

FIG. 41.—Transverse Section of Stomach.

a, Cylindrical Epithelium covering Papillæ. *b*, Peptic Glands. *c*, Muscularis Mucosæ. *d*, Submucous Tissue. *e*, Circular Muscular layer. *f*, Longitudinal Muscular layer. *g*, Peritoneum. (Klein.)

with spherical nuclei: they are known as the "*Chief Cells*." Scattered among them are a number of large oval granular cells, called the "*Parietal Cells*." The peptic glands secrete the essential elements of the gastric juice; they are found in the cardiac and central portions of the organ.

2d, The *Pyloric Glands* have ducts like the peptic glands, but larger; the epithelium lining them is of a similar kind. They are not so long, nor do they project so far down into the mucosa as do the cardiac glands. They are lined with a layer of columnar epithelium cells, and secrete a serous fluid. They are found, as their name implies, at the pyloric extremity of the organ.

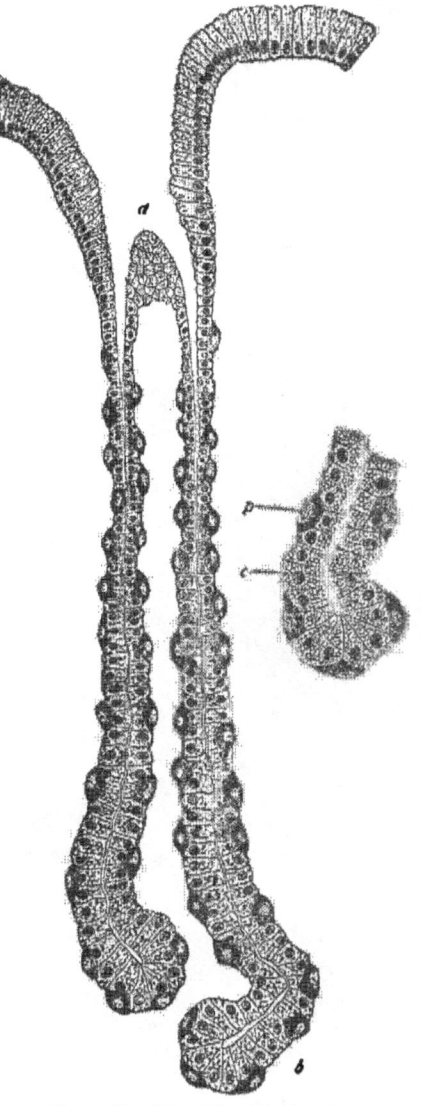

FIG. 42.—The Peptic Glands.

d, Duct and mouth. b, Fundus of one Lobule. p, Parietal Cell. c, Central Cell. (Klein.)

The *Submucous Connective Tissue* or areolar coat unites the mucosa loosely to the muscularis, and sustains the large branches of the nerves and lymphatics.

The *Muscular Coat* of the stomach is extremely thick. It consists of unstriped muscular fibres arranged in an inner circular, an outer longitudinal, and various oblique layers.

The *Serous Coat* is a part of the peritoneum and envelops the stomach save along the lines of the lesser and greater curvatures.

The *Bloodvessels* are very numerous, and as already stated, form plexuses around the glands of the mucosa. The *Lymphatics* and *Nerves* form similar plexuses.

The Small Intestine.

The Small Intestine possesses four coats: an internal mucous, a submucous, a muscular, and a serous coat.

The *Mucosa* is thinner than that of the stomach, but is also complicated in structure. Its surface has a velvety appearance from the presence of immense numbers of small projections called villi that stud its surface. Its connective-tissue basement substance is packed full of small tubular glands, the crypts of Lieberkühn; and much lymphoid tissue, aggregated in places into groups called *Solitary Glands* and *Peyer's Patches* is found there also. Smooth muscular fibres are present, and form a *Muscularis Mucosæ*. The epithelium is of the columnar variety.

The *Mucosa* contains:

Villi, which form closely set projections of the mucosa, like the "pile" of velvet. Of the same structure as the mucosa, they are composed of a basement substance covered with columnar epithelium. In the centre of each villus is a lacteal vessel, and around this vessel are muscular fibres derived from the muscularis mucosæ. A capillary bloodvessel forms a plexus in the villus; and much lymphoid tissue is present in the basement substance.

The *Crypts of Lieberkühn* are simple tubular glands lined with a columnar epithelium. Many of these cells are goblet cells, and secrete mucous.

The *Submucosa* is composed of fibrous connective tissue; it connects together the mucosa and the muscularis, and sus-

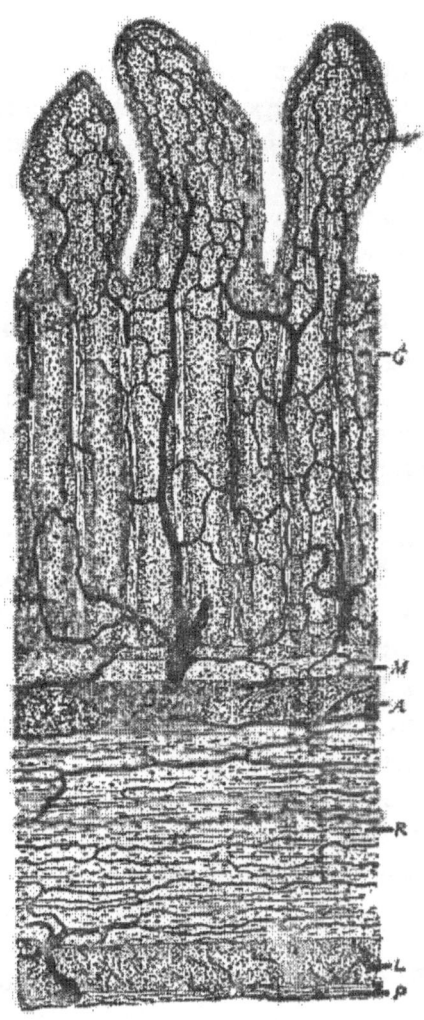

FIG. 43.—Vertical transverse section of Intestine, with injected Bloodvessels.

v, Villus. G, Glands of Lieberkühn
M, Muscularis Mucosæ. A, Areolar Coat.
R, Circular Muscular layer. L, Longitudinal Muscular layer. P, Peritoneal coat.
(Heitzman.)

tains the large vessels. The *Solitary Follicles* are aggregations of lymphoid tissue ; and *Peyer's Patches* are collections of solitary glands. The latter occur chiefly in the lower ileum.

The *Muscular Coat* consists of an inner circular and an outer longitudinal layer. In it are contained

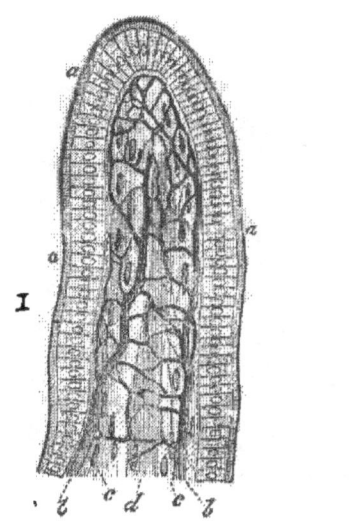 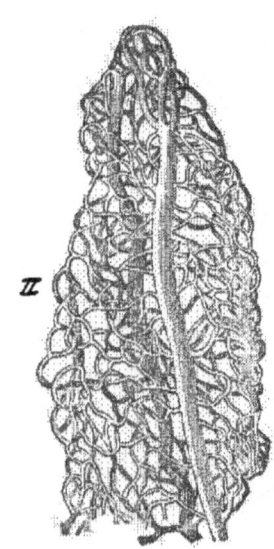

FIG. 44.—Intestinal Villi.

I, Villus (schematic). *a*, Epithelial covering. *b*, Capillary network. *c*. Longitudinal Muscular Fibres. *d*, Lacteal. (Leydig.) II, Capillary network of Villus. *a*, Venous trunk. *b*, Arterial trunk. (Frey.)

plexuses of non-medullated nerve fibres known as those of Auerbach and Meissner.

The *Serous Coat* is part of the peritoneum ; it invests the intestine save at the mesenteric attachment.

The *Bloodvessels* and the *Lymphatics* form plexuses at the base of the villi and around the crypts of Lieberkühn.

The Large Intestine.

The Large Intestine has a mucous, a submucous connective tissue, a muscular, and a serous coat.

The *Mucosa* is composed of a basement connective tissue covered with a columnar epithelium. It con-

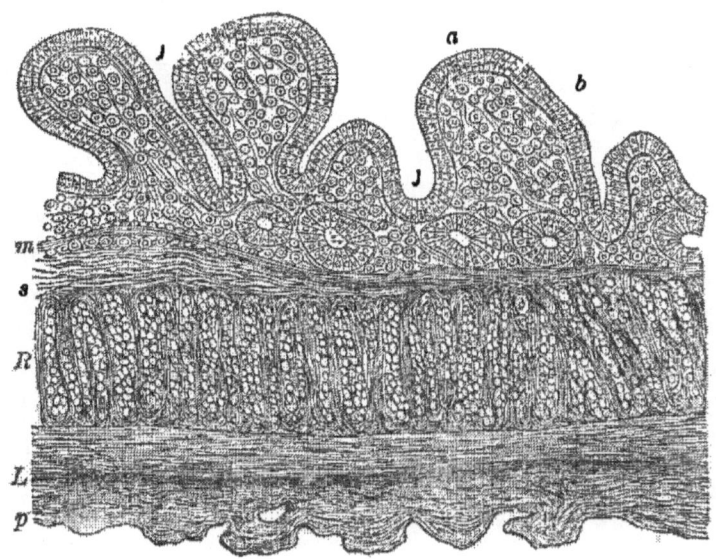

FIG. 45.—Section of Large Intestine of Rabbit.

J, Crypts of Lieberkühn. a, Epithelium. b, Mucosæ, m, Muscularis Mucosæ. s, Submucosæ. R, Circular Muscular layer. L, Longitudinal Muscular layer. p, Peritoneum.

tains a great many simple tubular glands similar to those of Lieberkuhn in the small intestine.

The *Submucosa* is of connective tissue and sustains the vessels and nerves.

The *Muscular Coat* is gathered up into three thick longitudinal bands which are apparently shorter than the other membranes, and so produce puckerings of the gut.

The *Serous Coat* is derived from the peritoneum : it is not present on the lower third of the large intestine.

Nerves, *Bloodvessels*, and *Lymphatics* are arranged the same as in the small intestine.

CHAPTER XV.

THE RESPIRATORY SYSTEM.

THE Respiratory apparatus consists of a number of small cavities lined with epithelium, and a system of tubes by which they communicate with the external air. These latter are the Larynx, Trachea, and Bronchi.

The Larynx.

The *Larynx* consists of a framework of cartilage lined with mucous membrane and provided with certain muscles.

1st, The *Mucous Membrane* of the larynx is lined internally with a ciliated epithelium, save on the epiglottis and the true vocal cord, where it is of the stratified pavement variety. The membrane itself is of delicate connective tissue containing a number of elastic fibres. Numerous mucous glands are imbedded in its substance, and supply the material to lubricate its surface.

2d, The *Cartilages* of the larynx are partly of the elastic and partly of the hyaline variety. Those of the Epiglottis, Santorini, and Wrisberg are of the former; those of the Thyroid, Cricoid, and Arytenoid are of the latter variety.

3d, The *Muscles* of the larynx are of the involuntary variety.

The *Blood Vessels* ramify in the mucosa. The *Lymphatics* are very large and abundant. Plexuses of non-medullated *Nerve Fibres,* with end-bulbs and taste-buds, are also present.

The Trachea.

The Trachea is a fibro-muscular tube whose walls are stiffened by C-shaped pieces of cartilage. It consists of:

1st, A *Mucous Membrane* composed of fibrous tissue, and containing the vessels and nerves. Small tubular mucous glands are abundant throughout it. Its surface is covered with a layer of ciliated epithelial cells, similar to that of the Larynx.

2d, An external *White Fibrous Connective-tissue* layer, investing and uniting together the cartilages.

3d, *Incomplete circles of Hyaline Cartilage*, which give rigidity to the tube. They are lined with a perichondrium that is continuous with the loose connective tissue of the fibrous layer in which they lie.

The Bronchi.

The *Bronchi* branch inside the lung dendritically into finer and finer tubes, until the *Ultimate Bronchi* open into the air spaces of the lung themselves. Their structure in a general way is the same as that of the trachea; but with certain important modifications. We have—

1st, A *Mucous Membrane* containing the vascular structures, mucous glands, etc., and covered with a columnar ciliated epithelium.

2d, A *Submucosa* composed of white fibrous and unstriped muscular tissue, and containing—

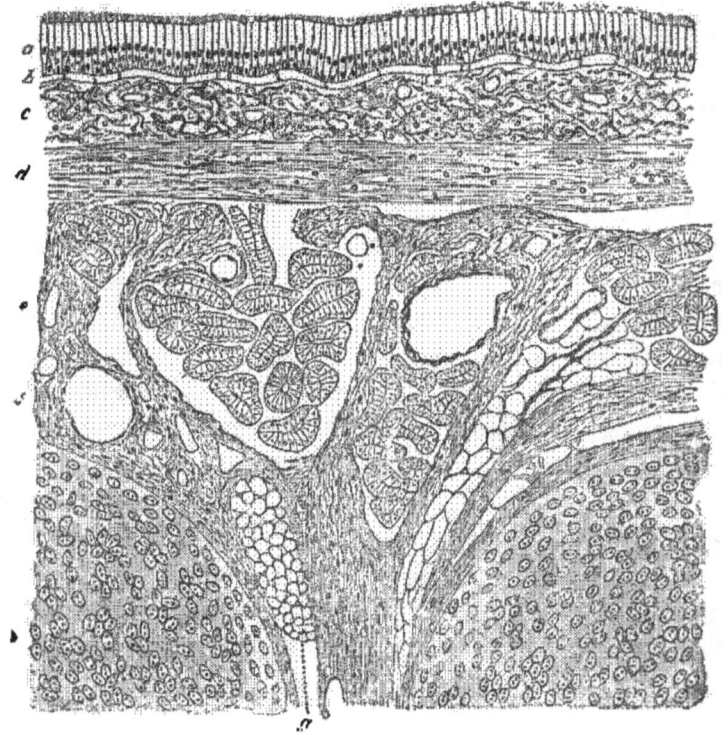

FIG. 46.—Longitudinal Section of Human Trachea.

a, Ciliated Epithelium. b, Basement Membrane. c, d, Mucous Membrane of Elastic Fibres, and containing the Vessels. e, Submucous Tissue containing Mucous Glands, Fat, &c. f, Fibrous Tissue investing and lining the Cartilages. g, Adipose Tissue. h, Cartilage. (Klein.)

3d, The *Cartilages*. These are hyaline, as in the trachea, but do not form complete C-shaped hoops. They are long or irregularly shaped plates placed at various points in the wall of the tube. They gradually diminish in size as we approach the smaller tubes, and are entirely absent in the smallest of them.

Fig. 47.—Diagramatic representation of the ending of a Bronchial Tube in sacculated Infundibulæ and vessels.

B, Terminal Bronchus. L, B, Lobular Bronchiole. A, Atrium.
I, Infundibulum. C, Alveoli or Air Cells. (Schaefer.)

Blood Vessels, *Lymphatics* and *Nerves* are very abundant in the submucous tissue of the bronchi.

The Lungs.

The *Lung* itself is composed of masses of polygonal vesicles known as the *Air Cells* or *Vesicles*. Each terminal bronchiole ends in a number of larger passages known as *Infundibulæ* and around these infundibulæ the air vesicles are grouped like bunches of grapes. The whole is bound together by connective tissue into *Lobules* and *Lobes*.

The *Air Vesicles* themselves are polygonal and quadrangular spaces, with a single layer of flattened epithelial cells. Immediately beneath this lies the *Capillary Plexus*, which is so abundant that it forms by far the greater part of the mass of the wall of the air vesicle. The capillary network itself is so close that the area occupied by the vessels is greater than the interspace between them. Thus two layers of epithelial cells separate the blood in the vessels from the air in the alveoli; the epithelium lining the alveoli, and the endothelial cells forming the wall of the cap-

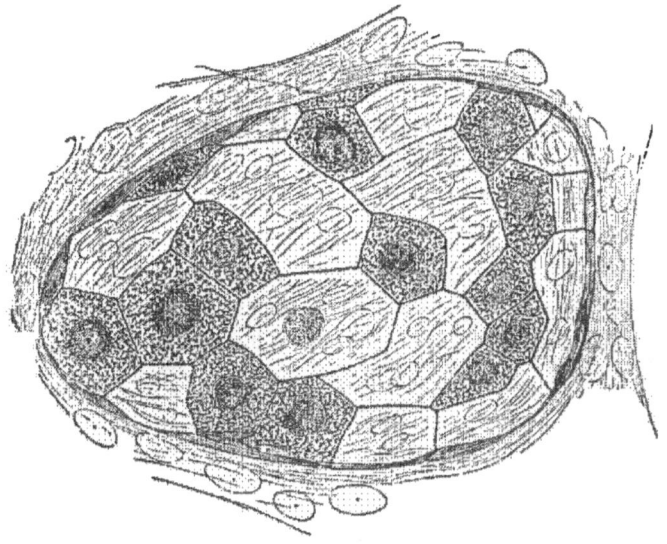

FIG. 48.—Alveolus of Lung of new born Child. (Schultze.)

illaries. Besides this only a minute amount of connective tissue is present in the walls of the alveoli.

Groups of air vesicles thus constituted, and surrounded closely by their dense net-capsules of capillaries, are clustered around the infundibulum in which each bronchiole terminates. Each such cluster forms a *Lobule* of the lung; and an aggregation of lobules forms a *Lobe*.

The *Pulmonary Artery* and the *Bronchial Arteries* both supply the lung: but whilst the latter is supplied

THE RESPIRATORY SYSTEM. 97

to the walls and the mucous membrane of the bronchial tubes, the former supplies the capillary network of the alveoli and is the functional artery of the organ. Both streams empty into the *Pulmonary Veins*, which pursue a separate course through the organ, and leave it at the *Hilum*.

The *Lymphatics* of the lung are abundant, and form two sets. One set accompanies the bronchial tubes,

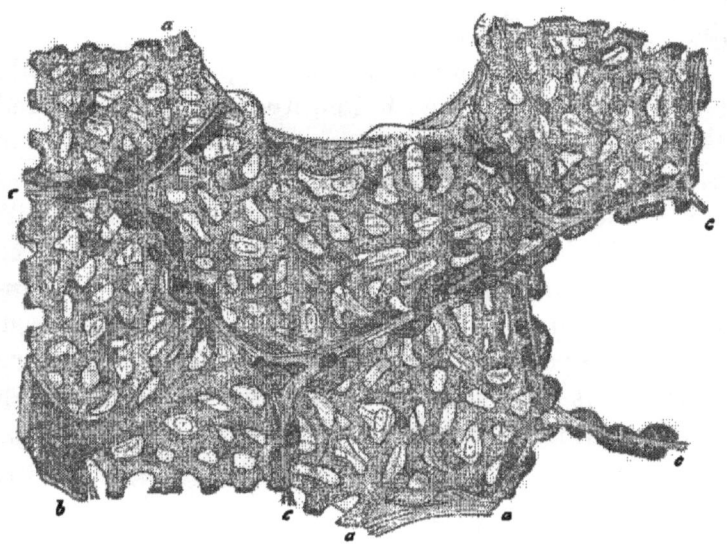

FIG. 49.—Section of Human Lung, injected.

a, a, Free margins of Alveoli. *b*, Small Artery. *c, c*, Alveolar Wall, seen on transverse section.

whilst the other ramifies in the interlobular and the interlobar connective tissue.

The *Pleura* surrounds the entire organ. It is a serous membrane, composed of a delicate connective tissue, and lined with a layer of flat endothelial cells.

CHAPTER XVI.

The Urinary System.

The Kidney.

THE Kidney is composed of a congeries of tubes lined with the epithelial cells that secrete the urine. A cross section of the organ shows it to be divided into two distinct portions, Cortical and Medullary.

The *Cortex* surrounds the deeper parts like a shell; it is closely marked with longitudinal gray and red stripes, being entirely composed of a dense mass of urinary tubules and vessels. Numerous minute red points, the *Malphigian Tufts*, are scattered through it.

The *Medulla* is enclosed, externally, by the cortex; internally it ends in one or more nipple-like prominences known as *Papillæ*, which project into the expanded opening of the ureter. The medullary substance is of a rather uniform grayish color, though a longitudinal striation can be observed on close observation. It contains no Malphigian tufts, and is composed of the larger collecting urinary tubes and their bloodvessels. At the apex of each papilla are a number of minute openings which are the orifices of the tubes.

At the point where the medullary and cortical portions of the kidney meet are seen the sections of large vessels, the *Arterial and Venous Arches*.

A fibrous *Capsule*, partly covered with a peritoneal coat, encloses the kidney. At the hilum a small amount of connective tissue accompanies the vessels into the interior, and forms the connective-tissue framework of the organ.

The *Uriniferous Tubules* are the parenchyma or essential secreting structures of the kidney. Each one consists of an apparently homogeneous basement membrane lined with a single layer of epithelial cells. Their course from their origins at the glomeruli to the apices of the papillæ is a tortuous one; doubling on themselves more than once both in the cortical and the medullary portion. Their diameter also varies greatly, and their epithelial lining is at one time cuboidal, at another time flat and scale-like. A variety of names have, therefore, been given to the various parts of the tubes, of which the most important are the following:

Bowman's Capsule is the dilated commencement of the uriniferous tubule in the cortex. It surrounds the plexus of capillary bloodvessels known as the Malphigian tuft, but it is not penetrated by it; it simply invaginates it and surrounds it with a double layer, and preserves its own cavity intact. The *Basement Membrane* of the capsule is covered with a layer of flat epithelial cells, which line the inner surface of the capsule completely, including that portion of it that

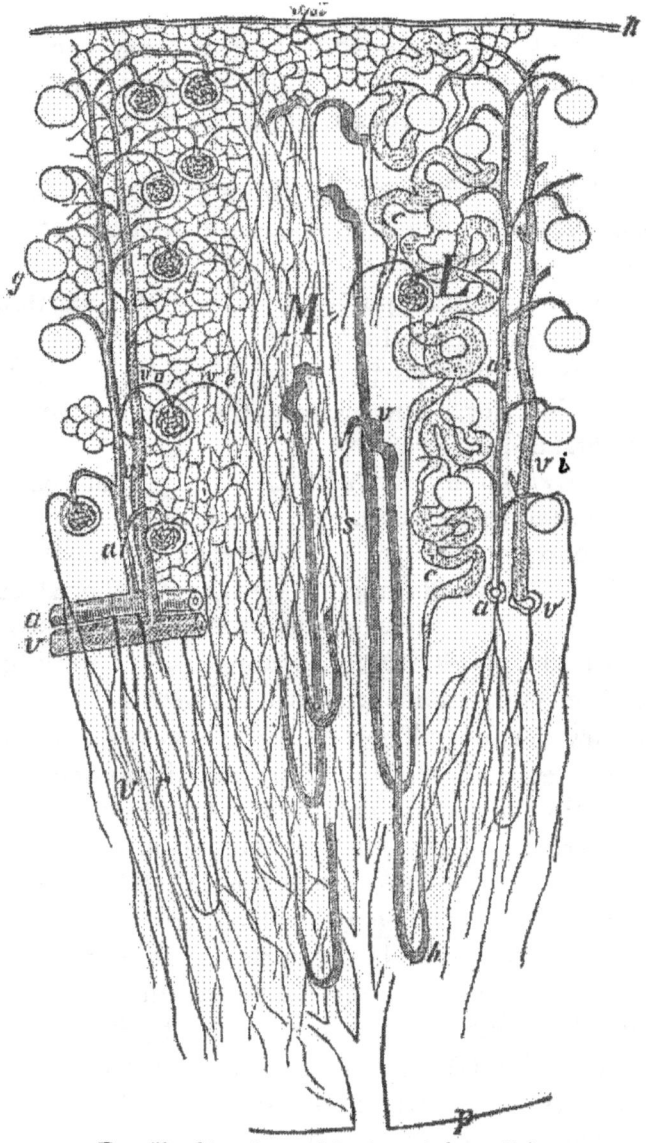

FIG. 50.—Structure of Kidney (schematic).

k, Capsule.   *p*, Papilla.   M, Medullary Vein.   L, Ligaments.
a, Arterial Arch.   *v*, Veinous Arch.   *a, i*, Interlobular Arteries.   *v. i*, Interlobular Veins.   *v, a*, Vasa Afferentia.   *g*, Glomeruli.   *v, e*, Vasa Efferentia.   *v, v*, Vasa Recti.   *c*, Tubuli Contorti.   *h*, Henle's Loop.   *v*, Interpolated Tube.   *s*, Collecting Tube.   (Orth.)

covers the leash of bloodvessels that it encloses. At the neck of the capsule begins the—

First Convoluted Tube. This is a wide sinuous tube, lined with large granular cells. It soon ends in a narrower tube, lined with a flatter epithelium which dips down into the medullary portion of the organ

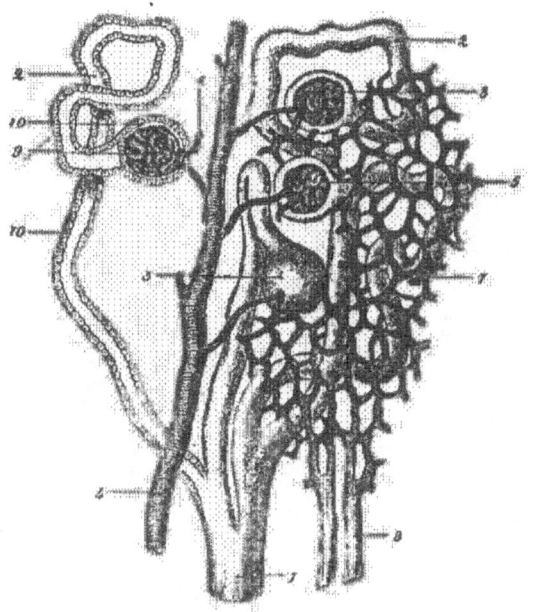

Fig. 51.—Kidney Structure (diagrammatic.)

1, Uriniferous Tubules in Medullary Substance. 2, Uriniferous Tubules in Cortex. 3, Termination of Uriniferous Tubules in Bowman's Capsule. 4, Arterial Trunk. 5, Glomerulus. 6, Afferent Vessels. 7, Vascular Network. 8, Efferent Vessels. 9, Vessels in the Glomerulus. 10, Lining Epithelium of Glomerulus. (Morel.)

to form *Henle's Loop*, of which the descending and ascending arms are sometimes enumerated as separate parts. The entire loop is narrow, and is lined with a regular cuboidal epithelium. When the tube reaches the cortex again it ramifies as the—

102 A MANUAL OF GENERAL HISTOLOGY.

Second Convoluted Tube. This is similar in structure to the first convoluted tube; by means of a short *Junctional Tubule* it joins the *Collecting Tubule.* This runs straight down through cortex and medulla to the excretory ducts at the apices of the papillæ, which are known as the *Ducts of Bellini*.

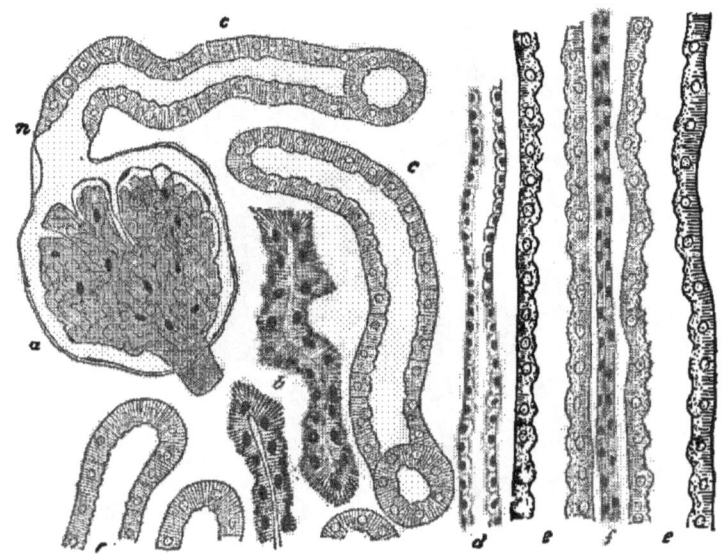

FIG. 52.—Tubules from a section of Dog's Kidney.

a, Capsule Enclosing Glomerulus. n, Neck of Capsule. c, c, Convoluted Tubes. b, Irregular Tubules. d, Collecting Tubes. e, e, Spiral Tubes. f, Part of Ascending Trunk of Henle's Loop.

The *Blood Vessels.* The *Renal Artery* enters the kidney at the hilum, passes up through the medullary substance to the line that divides the cortex from the medulla, and there forms a series of *Arterial Arches.* From the outer surface of these arches, branches pass straight up towards the cortex; they are the *Interlobular Arteries*, and form the minute red lines that are

THE URINARY SYSTEM. 103

visible in the cortical substance. From these arteries lateral twigs are given off at short intervals, which enter the *Bowman's Capsules* as the *Vasa Afferentes*. Each *Efferent Artery* enters the capsule at a point opposite the point of origin of the uriniferous tubule, breaks up into a network of capillaries, and then leaves

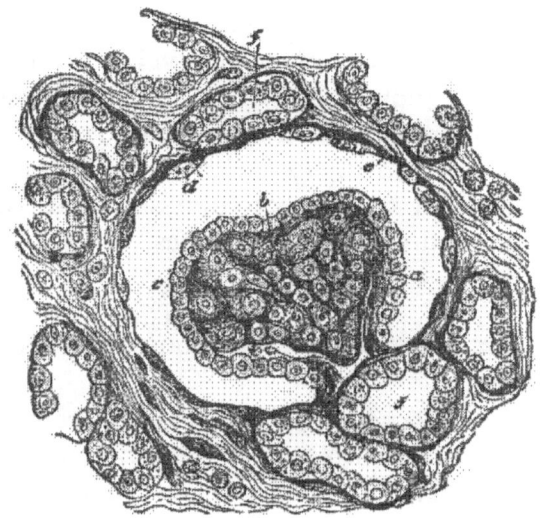

FIG. 53.—Section through Cortical Substance of Kidney of Human form.

a, Glomerulus. b, Tissue of Glomerulus. c, Epithelium covering Glomerulus. d, Flattened Epithelium lining Bowman's Capsule. e, Bowman's Capsule. f, Uriniferous Tubules, cross section. (Handbook.)

the capsule very near its point of entrance as the *Vas Efferens*. This capillary network is the *Glomerulus* or the *Malphigian Tuft*. As before stated, it does not penetrate the capsule of Bowman, but simply pushes it before it, and is covered by one of its layers. After leaving the capsule the Vas Efferens breaks up into a network of capillaries that lie among the closely packed convoluted tubules. The blood, now for the first time venous, is collected into small veins that join venous arches that run parallel to the arterial ones.

From the under surface of the arterial arches run down vessels known as the *Vasa Recta*, which supply the medullary portion of the kidney.

The *Renal Vein* runs along-side the renal artery. It forms venous arches parallel to the arterial ones, into whose convexity open the veins receiving the blood from the glomeruli, whilst the concave surface receives the vasa recta from the medulla.

The *Nerves* and *Lymphatics* of the kidney lie in the small amount of connective tissue that supports the secreting and vascular structures.

The Ureters.

These are musculo-membraneous tubes composed of three coats:

1st, The *Internal or Mucous Coat*, composed of areolar tissue lined with stratified epithelium.

2d, The *Middle or Muscular Coat*, consisting of an inner and outer longitudinal, and a middle layer of unstriped fibres.

3d, An *External Coat*, the *Adventitia*, formed of a thick connective tissue.

Bloodvessels and *Nerves* ramify in the external coat.

The Bladder.

The Bladder is very like the ureters in construction, but possesses a fourth coat.

1st, The *Internal or Mucous Coat*, is composed of areolar tissue with a lining of stratified epithelium.

2d, The *Middle Coat* is composed of unstriped

muscular tissue, and is very greatly developed. The fibres lay in large bands which may be divided into three coats: an internal circular, a middle oblique, and an external longitudinal.

3d, The *External Coat* is formed of dense white fibrous connective tissue.

4th, The last coat is formed by the *Peritoneum* which covers almost the entire surface of the organ. It is an areolar connective-tissue membrane, covered with a layer of pavement epithelium.

Nerves and *Vessels* run in the external and middle coats. In the muscularis are found large nerve ganglia.

The Urethra.

The Urethra consists of:

1st, An *Internal Coat* of vascular mucous membrane. The epithelium that covers the connective-tissue basis of the coat is columnar in most of the canal in the male, becoming squamous near the meatus; in the female it is scaly throughout. A number of oblique recesses occur in it, the *Lacunæ*. Mucous glands, known as the *Glands of Littré*, are scattered through it. Two small compound racemose glands, called *Cowper's Glands*, open into the bulbous portion of the urethra.

2d, The *Middle Muscular Coat* is composed of an internal longitudinal, and an external circular layer of unstriped fibres. It is covered in its anterior part by the spongy body, to be described under the male organs of generation.

3d, An *External Coat* of fibrous connective tissue.

The *Vessels* and *Nerves* ramify in the muscular coat.

CHAPTER XVII.

The Male Genital Organs.

The Testis.

THE *Testis* is a tubular gland which secretes the spermatozoa. It consists of a congeries of tubules lined with an epithelium from which the seminal elements are derived.

The *Tunica Albuginea* is a dense connective-tissue coat that envelops the entire organ and sends inward a number of incomplete septa that divide its interior into conical cavities. These *Septa* or *Trabeculæ* unite posteriorly to form a large mass of tissue known as the *Mediastinum* or *Corpus Highmori*. In the mole, hedgehog, bat, and man, the Highmorian body is peripheral; in the dog, cat, bull, etc., it is central, whilst the testicle of the rat and the mouse have no mediastinum at all.

The *Tunica Vaginalis* is a closed serous membrane that covers the tunica albuginea and is reflected onto the inner surface of the scrotal sac.

THE MALE GENITAL ORGANS. 107

The *Seminal Tubules* are convoluted tubes that lie in the cavities formed by the tunica albuginea. They are single tubes, though much twisted; and they straighten out as they approach the mediastinum. There they unite with other straight tubules, and

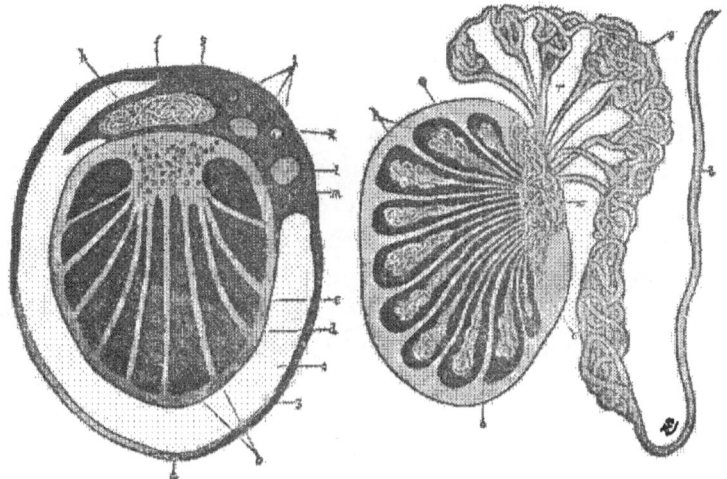

FIG. 54.—Transverse and vertical sections of Testicle.

a, Connective Tissue of Skin outside Tunica Vaginalis. *b*, Tunica Vaginalis, parietal layer. *c*, Cavity of Tunica Vaginalis. *d*, Visceral layer of Tunica Albuginea. *f*, Covering of Epididymis. *g*, Epididymis. *h*, Mediastinum Testis. *i*, Spermatic Artery branches. *k*, Spermatic Vein. *l*, Vas Deferens. *m*, Artery of Vas Deferens. *o*, Septa of Testicle. *p*, Tubuli Seminiferi in their Lobes. *q*, Straight Tubes. *r*, Vasa Efferentia. *u*, Coni Vasculosi.

form a network of intercommunicating vessels known as the *Rete Testis*. They pass out of the rete as a few straight tubules, and unite into the single tube of the epididymis.

Each *Tubule* is formed of a thick basement membrane, the *Membrana Propria*, on which lie several layers of epithelial cells. Of these only the innermost layers are concerned with the formation of zoosperms ; the outer layers are composed of cuboidal epithelium of the ordinary type. The inner layers, on the other hand, are known as *Spermatoblasts*, and are actively engaged in the process of change into spermatozoa. They become pear-shaped, and the nucleus recedes to the outer, sharper extremity. They then form elongated, club-shaped bodies, which are the young spermatozoa.

These immature spermatozoa are grouped together into peculiar fan-shaped masses, the heads, with the nuclei, being buried among the deeper epithelial layers and compressed by them ; while their other ends project like a fan into the lumen of the seminal tubule. The nucleus becomes the head, and the cell body becomes the middle piece of the zoosperm ; and from this there grows out a thin hair-like filament, the tail. When the development is complete the interstitial cement that holds the fan-shaped mass together is dissolved, and the spermatozoa are projected free into the tubule.

The *Spermatozoon* consists in man and the mammals of a head of varying shape, the nucleus of the spermatoblast ; a rod-shaped middle piece, the body or neck, formed of the body of the parent cell ; and a long, hair-like tail. During life the tail is in continual vibratile motion, like the cilium of a ciliated epithelium cell, and gives to the entire body a rapid oscillatory and propelling motion. Their shape and size differ greatly in the various animals. In man the head is oval, flattened, and pointed anteriorly. In the rat the head is long and recurved anteriorly ; the neck is long and has a closely-wound spiral filament encircling it. In the newt the head is pike-shaped and a filament encircles the tail for a considerable portion of its length. The horse and sheep has spermatozoa

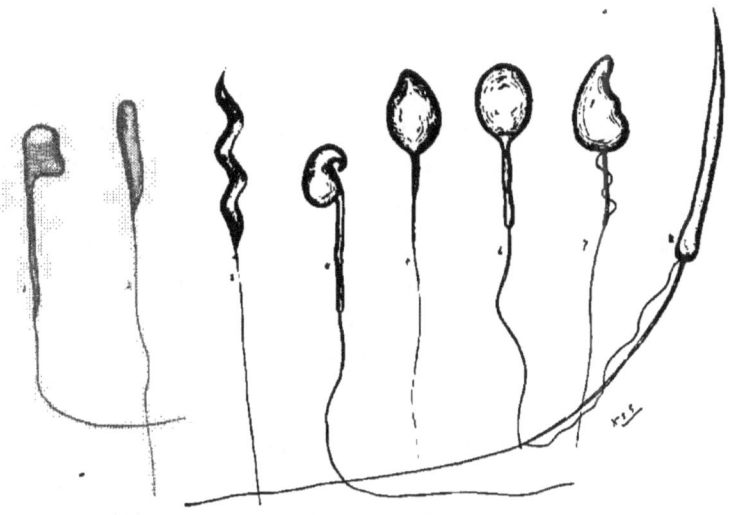

FIG. 55.—Zoosperms.

1, Hedge Hog. 2, Frog. 3, Finch. 4, Field Mouse. 5, Man. 6, Sheep. 7, Horse. 8, Newt.

very like that of man; but in the former animal a small spiral filament encircles the neck and the upper part of the tail.

The Epididymis.

The *Epididymis* is attached to the posterior surface of the testicle, and is composed of a single, greatly convoluted tube into which the efferent testicular ducts have united. A mass of connective tissue, sustaining the vessels and the nerves, binds the tubal mass into an oval body.

The tube of the epididymis is very similar to a seminal tubule. There is a membrana propria, but only a single layer of large nucleated and ciliated epithelial cells lines it. It ends in a single larger tube known as the *Vas Deferens*, an expansion of which forms the *Vesicula Seminalis*.

The Prostate.

The *Prostate* is a gland composed of ducts lined with a columnar epithelium. The ducts are wavy branched tubes that gradually coalesce into a few chief tubes and open into the urethra at the base of the colliculus seminalis. The framework that supports the tubes differs from that of other glands in that it is mostly composed of unstriped muscular fibres, and contains but little connective tissue.

The Penis.

The *Penis* is composed of three masses of erectile or cavernous tissue, viz. : the *Corpora Cavernosa*, one on each side, and the *Corpus Spongiosum* lying between them. Each corpus cavernosum is enclosed in an albugineous covering of dense connective tissue, from which trabeculi run inwards and form the cavernous spaces of the erectile tissue. The sinuses are lined with a single layer of endothelial cells, and are directly continuous with the capillary bloodvessels. When the penis is flaccid the blood passes directly from the capillaries of the corpus into the small efferent veins ; during erection it flows into and fills the large cavernous sinuses, only later and more slowly flowing out through the veins. The *Corpus Spongiosum* is composed of a cavernous tissue similar to that of the corpora cavernosa, and a number of large veins. These are bound together by connective tissue and unstriped muscular fibre. It undergoes erection by

THE MALE GENITAL ORGANS. 111

the filling of the large veins and the cavernous sinuses with blood. It surrounds the anterior portion of the urethra, and ends in front in an expansion known as the *Glans*.

The *Glans Penis* has an external covering of mucous membrane, the surface of which is closely set

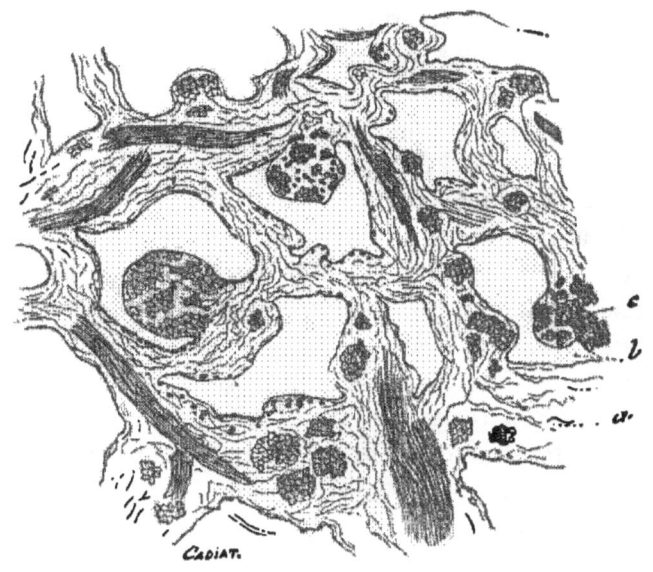

FIG. 56.—Section of Erectile Tissue.

a, Trabeculi of Connective Tissue with Elastic Fibres and bundles of plain Muscular Fibres (c).   b, Venous Spaces.

with papillæ. These *Papillæ* contain loops of blood-vessels and plexuses of non-medulated nerve fibres which connect with *End Bulbs*, previously described, in the deeper layers. These give to the organ its exquisite sensibility.

CHAPTER XVIII.

The Female Genital Organs.

The Ovary.

THE *Ovary* is a gland composed of epithelium arranged in alveoli, and supported by a fibrous framework. It is peculiar in that the alveoli have no excretory ducts, but discharge their contents by a periodic rupture at the surface of the organ.

The *Stroma* or *Interstitial Tissue* of the ovary is a dense white fibrous connective tissue, mingled with a considerable amount of unstriped muscular fibre. It is abundantly supplied with bloodvessels and lymphatics, which form capillary plexuses around the parenchymatous alveoli. The surface of the organ is covered with a single layer of cylindrical epithelium, the serous peritoneal covering being absent. These surface epithelial cells have an important relation to the secreting structure of the organ.

The *Parenchyma* or essential secreting structure of the ovary consists of a large number of vesicles of varying size scattered through the stroma. These are the *Graafian Follicles*. They differ greatly in size; some, in the deeper portions of the organ being $\frac{1}{20}$ of an inch in diameter, whilst many of the peripheral ones are so small as to be microscopic.

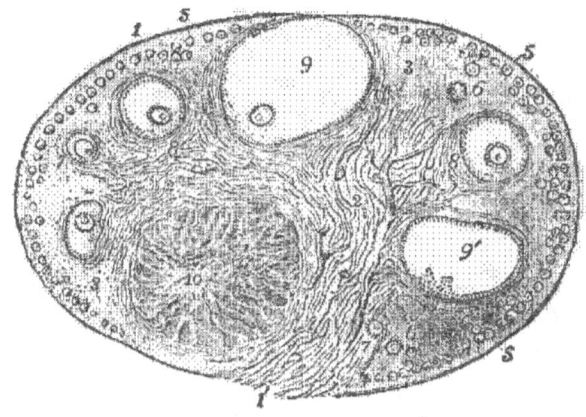

Fig. 57.—Section of Ovary of Cat.

1, Outer covering and free border of Ovary. 1¹, Attached border. 2, Central Ovarian Stroma, showing a Fibrous and Vascular structure. 3, Peripheral Stroma. 4, Bloodvessels. 5, Graafian Follicles in their earliest stage lying near the surface. 6, 7, 8, More advanced Follicles which are embedded more deeply in the Stroma. 9, An almost mature Follicle containing the Ovum in its deepest part. 9¹, Follicle with Ovum fallen out. 10, Corpus Luteum, (Schwann.)

Each Graafian follicle is situated in a cavity formed by a hardened layer of the stroma of the organ called the *Theca Folliculi*, and containing an abundant capillary network. This is lined with a cuboidal epithelium called the *Membrana Granulosa*, which in the smaller and younger follicles is single, but in the older ones is several rows deep and encloses a certain amount of colorless fluid, the *Liquor Folliculi*. At one point in the interior of the follicle the epithelium cells are heaped up into the *Germ-hill* or *Discus Proligerous*; embedded in this is the *Ovum*. As the follicle approaches maturity the fluid increases in quantity, and probably in part causes the final rupture.

The *Ovum* itself is a specialized epithelial cell of the membrana granulosa. It is large, spheroidal, and measures when mature $\frac{1}{120}$ of an inch. It is covered externally with a thick striated membrane, the *Zona Pellucida*. Inside this is the *Vitellus* or *Yolk*, filled with fatty or albuminous granules; it represents the protoplasm of the cell. Situated usually excentrically in the yolk is a large round nucleus, the *Germinal Vesicle*; and inside this is a well-marked nucleolus, the *Germinal Spot*.

The *Graafian Follicles* are derived from the surface epithelium that covers the organ. Processes of epithelium cells grow down in early life into the stroma of the organ, and are then cut off by the rapidly developing connective tissue. As these follicles mature their epithelium multiplies, fluid accumulates, and they approach the surface of the organ. Finally they rupture, usually at a menstrual epoch, and the ovum with a portion of the fluid and the follicular epithelium is discharged. A hemorrhage from the capillaries of the follicle wall then fills the cavity with a blood clot. This forms the *Corpus Luteum*, whose future development depends upon whether the ovum extruded has been impregnated or not. The extravasated blood goes through the ordinary changes. It coagulates, the serum is absorbed, the red cells disintegrate, and the hæmaglobin, taken up by the surrounding parts, changes into hæmatoidin crystals and black pigment. The epithelium left behind proliferates for a time and then dies; it undergoes fatty degeneration, and thus forms the yellow mass from which the body receives its name. The entire mass is finally absorbed, and only a pigmented cicatrix remains to mark its site.

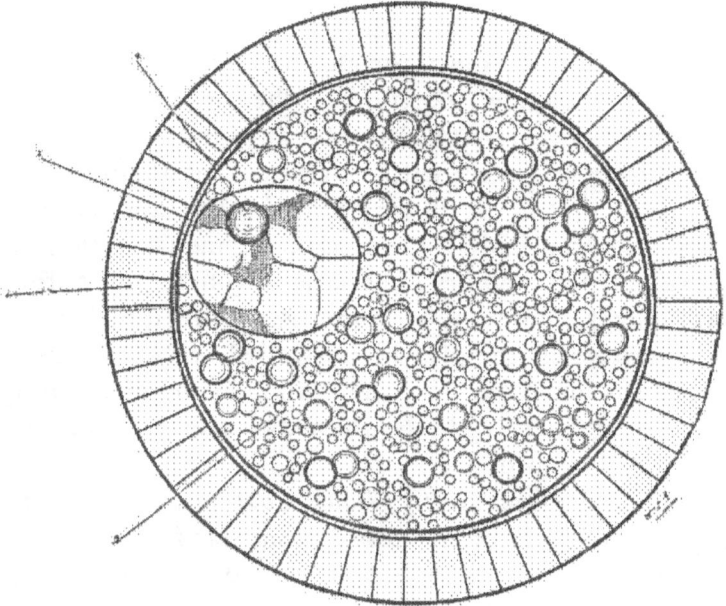

FIG. 58.— Semi-diagrammatic representation of Mammalian Ovum.
1, Zona Pellucida. 2, Vitellus. 3, Germinal Vesicle. 4, Germinal Spot.

The difference between the corpus luteum of the impregnated and the unimpregnated ovum is simply one of degree: in the former case the residual epithelium germinates during the entire period of pregnancy and finally forms a large fatty mass; in the latter, proliferation stops in a few days, and the small accumulation soon passes through the degenerative stages.

The Uterus.

The Uterus is composed essentially of a number of layers of smooth muscular fibres, with a small amount of interstitial connective tissue binding them together. We distinguish three coats:

1st, The *Mucous or Internal Coat* is composed of thick connective tissue, covered with a columnar ciliated epithelium. Near the os, however, the epithelium gradually changes into the squamous type which covers the vaginal portion of the organ. A large number of simple, straight tubular glands, the *Glandulæ Uterinæ*, lined with a ciliated epithelium, are embedded in it. It is very abundantly supplied with blood and lymphatic vessels. During menstruation the entire mucous membrane becomes swollen, and gorged with blood and lymph; and the epithelium, both of the surface and the glands, is swelled. By rupture or diapedesis or both, the menstrual blood containing large quantities of both glandular and surface epithelial cells is produced.

2d, The *Muscular or Middle Coat* is composed of a number of layers of unstriped muscular fibres. They are not very distinct, but it is usual to enumerate three: an internal transverse, a middle longitudinal, and an outer irregular layer. It is the development of this middle coat during pregnancy that causes the great increase in bulk of that organ at that time.

3d, The *Serous or Outer Coat* is of the peritoneum. It does not completely invest the organ, covering only the greater part of the fundus. The vascular supply of the uterus is very abundant, especially the veins. These form large irregular sinuses in the muscular layer, making it a species of cavernous tissue.

The Fallopian Tubes.

The Fallopian Tubes have three coats:

1st, The *Internal Coat* is of vascular mucous membrane, lined with ciliated epithelium.

2d, The *Middle Coat* is composed of an internal circular and an external longitudinal layer of unstriped muscular fibres.

3d, The *External Coat* is serous, and is derived from the peritoneum.

The Vagina.

The Vagina is a musculo-membraneous tube consisting of three coats:

1st, The *Internal Coat* is of plicated mucous membrane of connective tissue lined with a thick, stratified pavement epithelium. Papillæ project from the mucous membrane into the epithelium over its whole surface. The bloodvessels are so abundant as to give it somewhat the character of cavernous erectile tissue.

2d, The *Middle Coat* is muscular, and consists of an inner circular and an outer longitudinal layer of unstriped muscular fibres.

3d, The *Outer Coat* is of dense connective tissue.

The vagina is abundantly supplied with vessels and lymphatics. The mucosæ contain many nerve plexuses and end-bulbs.

The Nymphæ, Clitoris and Vestibulum.

These organs are formed of a cavernous tissue similar to the analogous organs, the corpora cavernosa in the male. They are covered with a thick mucous membrane clothed with stratified epithelium. They contain large sebaceous glands, an abundant vascular network, and end-bulbs.

CHAPTER XIX.

The Skin.

THE Skin consists of three chief layers: the Epidermis, or epithelial layer; the Corium or true skin; and the Subcutaneous Connective Tissue. The Epidermis is further divided into a Horny and a Mucous Layer, the latter containing portions known as the Stratum Lucidum and the Stratum Granulosum. The true skin contains papillæ, tactile, vascular, and lymphatic organs, and sweat and sebaceous glands. Finally, certain appendages—the hair, nails, horns, etc., are connected with the various layers; the whole forming a structure of considerable complexity.

1st, The *Epidermis* is the superficial layer of the skin, and consists of a number of layers of stratified epithelium. The upper ones (the horny layers) are hard and dry and form the protecting surface; the deeper ones (the rete layers) are soft and protoplasmic.

The *Stratum Cornium* or *Horny Layer of the Epidermis* consists of thin, transparent, scale-like epithelial cells, without visible nuclei, and closely packed together. Its lowest layer consists of transparent cells, and is known as the *Stratum Lucidum*.

The *Rete Mucosum* or *Rete Malphigi*, or the *Rete*, is the deeper succulent layer of the epidermis. It consists of nucleated, more or less cylindrical epithelial cells, which cover the papillæ of the corium underneath and fill out the hollows between them. Its superficial layer, which is in contact with the stratum lucidum of the epidermis, is composed of flattened granular cells, and is known as the *Stratum Granulosum*. The pigment of colored skins occurs as granules in the cells of the deeper layers of the rete.

The relative amounts of the corneous layer and the rete differ in the various parts of the body. In the palms and soles the horny layer is very thick, whilst in other parts the rete is predominant. The cells of the deeper layers of the rete grow and multiply, and push up the superficial cells. These become more and more horny, lose their nuclei, and are finally cast off as the insensible desquamation of the surface of the body.

2d, The *Corium* or *Cutis Vera*, or *True Skin*, is composed of dense bundles of white fibrous connective tissue, with a considerable number of elastic fibres. It varies in texture in different parts of the body. Its surface is covered with papillæ, on which and between which are the deeper layers of the rete mucosum. These papillæ contain looped capillary lymphatic vessels and bloodvessels; and some, especially those on the palms and fingers, and the soles and toes, contain tactile organs.

3d, The *Subcutaneous Connective Tissue* is continuous with the lower layer of the corium. Like it, it consists of interlacing bundles of white fibrous tissue,

120 A MANUAL OF GENERAL HISTOLOGY.

but arranged in a more open network. It binds the skin to the subjacent tissues; but the closeness of this union varies greatly in different parts of the body.

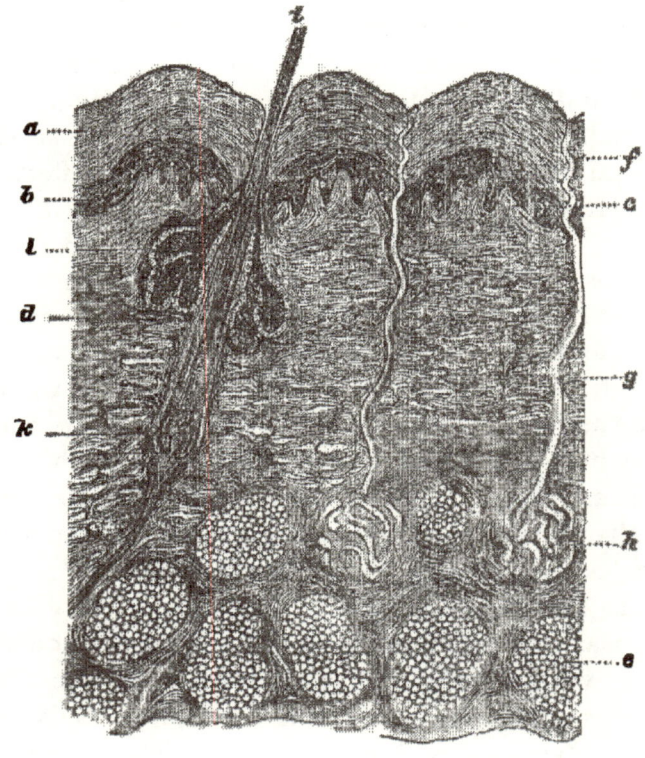

FIG. 59.—Diagrammatic perpendicular section through normal Skin.

a, Epidermis. b, Rete Malphigi. c, Papillary layer. d, Corium. e, Panniculus Adiposus. f, Spirally bent end of Excretory Sweat Duct. g, Staight part of Excretory Duct of Sweat Gland. h, Coil of Sweat Duct. i, Hair Shaft. k, Root of Hair. l, Sebaceous Gland. (After Neumann.)

It also supports the main branches of the vessels and the nerves. Much of it is developed into fatty connective tissue, and forms the *Panniculus Adiposus*.

THE SKIN.

The *Bloodvessels* of the skin run in the subcutaneous connective tissue; branches are sent up to the papillæ, the sweat and sebaceous glands, etc., and form capillary networks in and around those structures. The epidermis contains no vessels.

The *Lymphatics* are extremely abundant in all the layers and unite to form large branches in the subcutaneous tissue.

The *Nerves* end in networks between the epithelial cells of the rete. In the regions where the sense of touch is especially developed, as in the palm of the hand, the sole of the foot, and the skin of the penis, the nerves end in *Pacinian Corpuscles* in the papillæ (see Chap. VIII.). *Tactile* or *Meissner's Corpuscles* are also found in these situations.

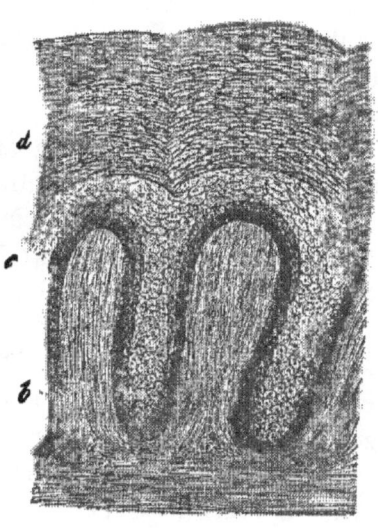

FIG. 60.—Skin of Negro, vertical section.

a, a, Cutaneous Papillæ. *b,* Pigment layer, *c* Rete. *d,* Corium layer.

The *Sweat* or *Sudoriparous Glands* are coiled tubes imbedded in the corium and the upper part of the subcutaneous connective tissue, and opening on the surface of the skin by a minute duct that pierces the epidermis. They are found over the whole skin, but are most abundant in the palms and soles. The secreting tube of delicate membrane is lined with a single layer of cuboidal epithelium. This is coiled into a ball that measures ₜ₀ to ₁₀ of an inch in diameter. The excretory tube that passes up through the epidermis is composed of the structureless basement membrane alone. Each gland is surrounded by a special cluster of bloodvessels and receives nerve filaments.

The *Sebaceous Glands* are small saccular glands connected with the hair follicles. They vary greatly in size, and are lined with a large nucleated epithelium. The oily *Sebum* that lubricates the skin is the product of the disintegration of these cells.

The *Ceruminous Glands* of the ear are constructed like the sebaceous glands. The protoplasm of the epithelial cells lining them contains a yellowish-brown pigment similar to that of the wax secreted by them.

The *Nails* are thickenings of the stratum lucidum of the epidermis over a specially modified corium. This latter forms the *Matrix* of the nail, and it is longitudinally ridged as well as papillated, like the rest of the corium. The body of the nail rests upon this bed, whilst the *Root* of the organ is fixed in a shallow pocket of skin, the corium of which forms the bed of the nail. The nail itself is composed of closely packed scale-like epithelial cells. The growth of the nail takes place from the *Lunulum*, which is the thicker portion of the nail embedded in the matrix.

The *Hairs.* Over the whole skin, save on the palms and soles, are scattered great numbers of cylindrical depressions or involutions of the epidermis, the *Hair Follicles.* In each of them is implanted a peculiar structure composed of epithelial cells—a hair. Three varities of hair are found. One kind is very minute, is scattered over all the so-called non-hairy parts of the body, and is known as the *Lanugo Hair*. Another variety is much larger and stiffer, and forms the *Ordinary Hair*. The difference between them, however, is merely one of size; their structure is exactly the same. The *Tactile Hairs* are the larger and deeply seated ones which occur about the lips in various animals, the dog, cat, rabbit, rat, etc. The blood channels in the papillæ of these hairs are so large as to form an erectile cavernous tissue. The nerve supply is very abundant, and they contain tactile corpuscles.

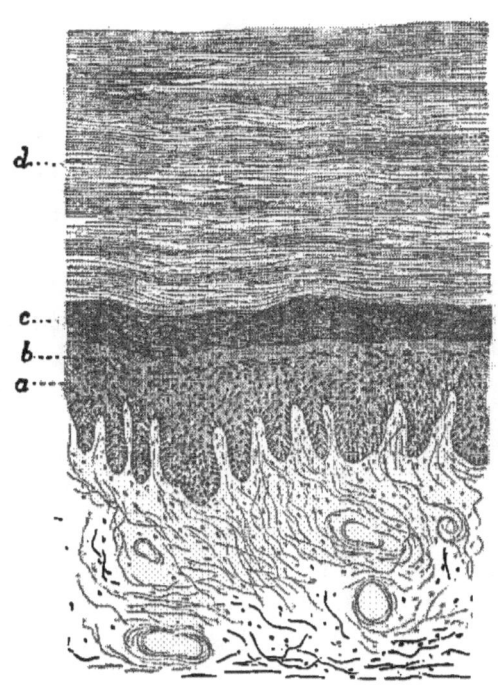

FIG. 61.—Vertical section through Nail and Bed.

a, Stratum Malphigi of Nail-bed b, Stratum Granulosum of Nail-bed. c, Deep layers of Nail substance. d, Superficial layers of same. (Klein.)

The *Hair Follicle* is a cylindrical involution of the epidermis and corium that extends obliquely downwards through the skin, and in the largest and coarsest hairs may reach far down into the subcutaneous tissue. It has three coats:

124 A MANUAL OF GENERAL HISTOLOGY.

1st, The *Outer Coat* is composed of the condensed connective tissue of the corium; at the base of the follicle it forms a projection known as the *Papilla*.

2d, The *Middle Coat* is called the *Hyaline* or *Glassy Membrane;* it corresponds to the superficial layer of the corium.

3d, The *Inner Coat* is the *External Root Sheath ;* it consists of a number of layers of stratified epithelium, and is the incurvated Rete Malphigi.

All three coats are present in the papilla that projects into the cavity of the follicle at its base. The hair itself grows by the multiplication of the soft cells of the external root sheath that cover the papilla. They become elongated, are pushed upwards, and become modified into the various substances that constitute the hair itself.

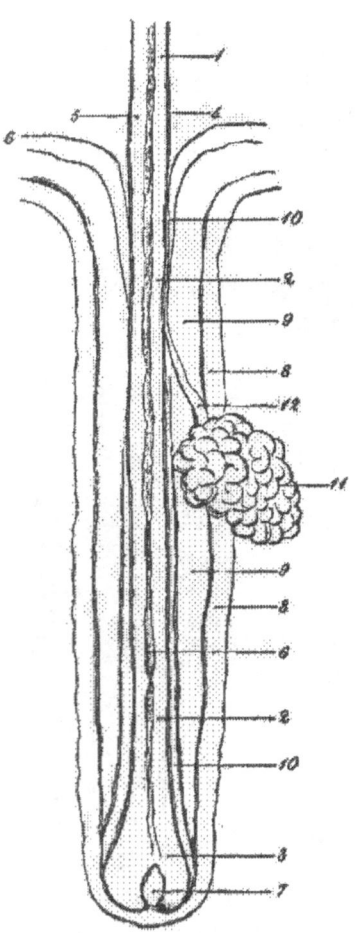

FIG. 62.—Hair (semi-diagrammatic).

1, Lower part of Shaft. 2, Root. 3, Bulb. 4, Outer coat of Hair. 5, Cortical substance of Hair. 6, Medullary Canal. 7, Papilla. 8, Dermic coat. 9, Outer Root Sheath. 10, Inner Root Sheath. 11, Sebaceous Gland with, 12, Its Excretory Duct.

Hence, the extraction of a hair from its follicle is followed by the growth of a new hair in its place, and is little better than cutting or shaving it off. Only the destruction of the hair follicle itself prevents its reappearance.

The *Hair* itself is composed of a cylindrical *Shaft* situated in the upper part of the follicle and extending beyond the surface, and a bulbous *Root*, situated in the lower part of the follicle and embracing the papilla. It is composed of:

1st, The *Medulla*, a dark substance consisting of angular separated cells that contain minute air bubbles, which cause its dark appearance. It is not present in the colorless lanugo hairs. In the lower animals it is often curiously arranged.

2d, A *Fibrous Material*, pigmented and horny, which forms the main part of the shaft of the hair. By means of acids it can be separated into long fibrillated cells, the nuclei of which are still visible.

3d, A *Cuticle*, composed of a layer of delicate imbricated scales that covers the entire hair. The cells differ greatly in different animals, and give to the various hairs their characteristic appearance.

4th, An *Internal Root Sheath* composed of horny cuboidal cells. It covers the root of the hair, being in contact with the external root sheath of the follicle. It has been divided into a number of layers, known as those of Huxley, Henle, etc.

The *Color* of hair depends on the amount of pigment granules in the medulla and fibrous material of the shaft.; the more pigment the darker the hair. Red hairs have a diffuse, lighter pigment. Very fair and white hair, as of albinos, has no pigment at all.

CHAPTER XX.

The Eye.

THE eye is composed of the terminal expansion of the Optic Nerve, with various supporting and moving structures, arrangements for regulating the amount of light admitted, etc. It is an organ of the greatest complexity, and its full description would far exceed our present limits. Its parts, briefly enumerated, are as follows:

1st, The *Conjunctiva* is a mucous membrane, and covers only the anterior free portion of the eyeball. It is composed of fibrous connective tissue containing networks of bloodvessels. Over the sclerotic portion the epithelium is of the short columnar variety; but on the cornea it becomes pavement epithelium. Lymphatics and nerve fibres are abundant; the latter form plexuses and have a number of end bulbs attached to them (see Chap. VIII).

2d, The *Sclera* or the *Sclerotic Coat* is the connective tissue envelope that encloses the posterior and middle two-thirds of the eyeball. It is composed of

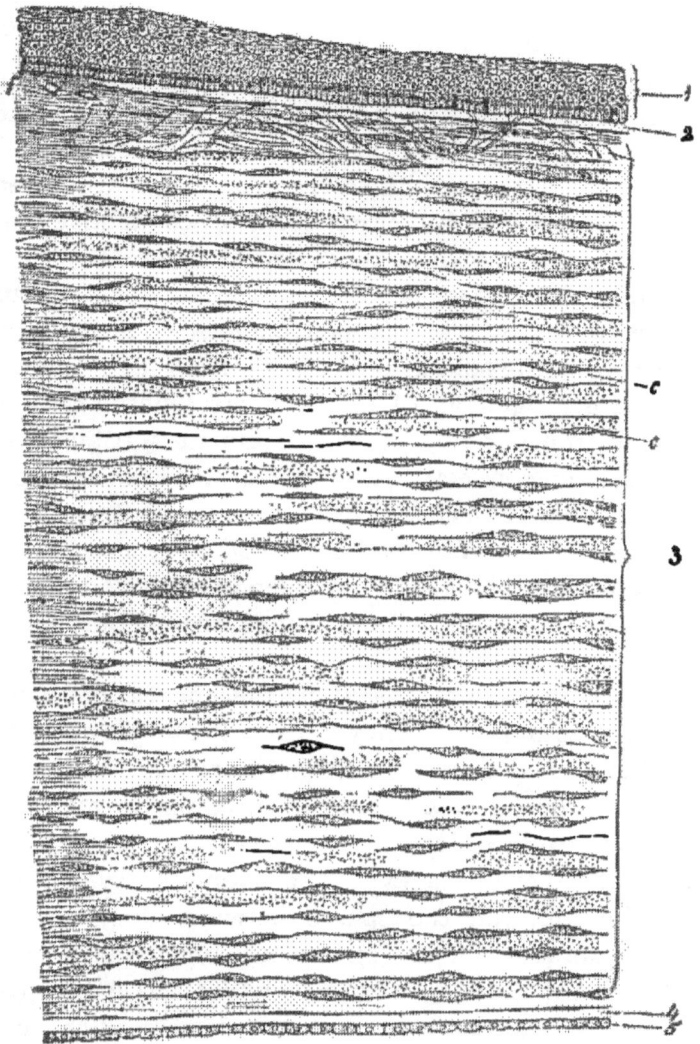

Fig. 63.—Vertical section of Human Cornea.

1, Epithelium. 2, Anterior Elastic Lamina. 3, Substantia Propria. 4, Posterior Elastic Lamina. 5, Epithelium of Anterior Chamber. c. Corneal Corpuscles. f. Bloodvessels. (Waldeyer.)

densely interwoven connective tissue with some elastic fibres ; and by its stiffness and rigidity preserves the globular shape of the organ. Minute fibres pass from it to the conjunctiva outside and the choroid coat within, uniting them firmly to one another. The point at the rear of the sclera where the optic nerve enters is covered by a network of connective-tissue fibres, and is known as the *Lamina Cribrosa*.

3d, The *Cornea* closes up the anterior circular orifice in the sclera. It is a connective-tissue membrane like the sclera, but differs from it in the more regular arrangement of the connective-tissue cells, the greater transparency of the basement substance, etc. Two elastic connective-tissue laminæ, known respectively as the *Anterior Elastic Lamina* and the *Posterior Elastic Lamina* or *Membrane of Descemet*, line the substance proper of the cornea in front and behind ; and a layer of epithelium covers the whole both in front and in the rear.

Bloodvessels are absent in the cornea, but nerves are very abundant. They form delicate plexuses that end between the anterior epithelial cells.

4th, The *Choroid* is a connective-tissue membrane which is divided into four distinct layers. It is the vascular layer of the eye. Each one is covered with endothelium, and the spaces between them are lymphatic sinuses. The outermost one, next to the sclera, is the *Lamina Supra-choroidea*. It is composed of connective tissue and elastic fibres, with many irregular pigmented cells. Next is the *Layer of Haller*, a similar membrane with many minute bloodvessels and pigment cells. Then comes the *Choriocapillaris*, composed almost entirely of a dense network of capillary bloodvessels. Most internally we have the *Lamina Vitrea*, of delicate, finely striated connective tissue.

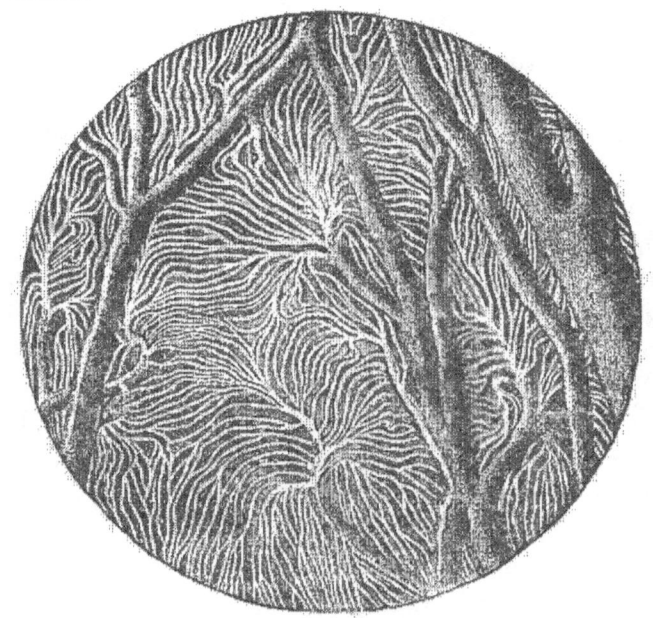

FIG. 64.—Injected Bloodvessels of Choroid. (Sappey.)

5th, *The Iris.* This is the part of the vascular coat that hangs in front of the lens. Like the choroid it is composed of connective tissue with elastic fibres and bloodvessels; but its pigment cells are of various colors instead of being uniformly black. Around the pupillary opening in the centre lies a band of smooth muscular fibres, the *Sphincter Pupillæ*; in certain animals, but not in man, other bands of similar fibres pass from the centre to the periphery of the organ, forming the *Dilator Pupillæ*. A thick layer of pigmented epithelium covers the back of the iris, called the *Uvea*.

6th, The *Retina* is one of the most complicated structures in the body. It consists of a connective-tissue framework that supports the terminal nerve elements of the optic nerve. Not less than ten layers are to be distinguished, as follows:

a, The *Internal Limiting Membrane* is a delicate connective-tissue membrane that lines the interior of the retina, and is in contact with the hyaloid membrane of the vitreous humor.

b, The *Layer of Nerve Fibres* is formed by the expansion of the fibres of the nerve after they have pierced the coats of the eyeball. They have lost their medullary sheath, and they gradually thin out as they reach the anterior part of the retina.

c, The *Layer of Nerve Cells* is composed of large unipolar or bipolar nerve cells, the axis-cylinder processes of which are continuous with the nerve fibres of the preceding layer.

d, The *Internal Molecular Layer* is thick and resembles the gray matter of the nerve centres. It is composed of axis-cylinders from the preceding layer, with nuclei and many granules.

e, The *Internal Nuclear Layer* is composed of bipolar nerve cells with large nuclei. Their posterior poles run into the internal molecular layer (*d*) behind them and form an arborization there. Their external poles run into the outer molecular layer (*f*), form similar plexuses, and reach the external limiting membrane (*h*), and there end in a free (*f*) pointed extremity.

f, The *External Molecular Layer* is formed chiefly by arborization of the fibres from the internal nuclear layer.

THE EYE. 131

g, The *External Nuclear Layer* is composed chiefly of nerve cells. It, with—

h, The *Membrana Limitans Externa*, and

i, The *Layer of Rods and Cones* are composed of structures that are continuous through the three layers, and are to be mentioned together. There is here a combination of nerve tissue and epithelium of a structure entirely too complicated to be even briefly described here. The rods are continuous with the axes of the nerve cells of the external nuclear layer; the cones are also connected with the nerve elements within, and terminate anteriorly in free pointed extremities.

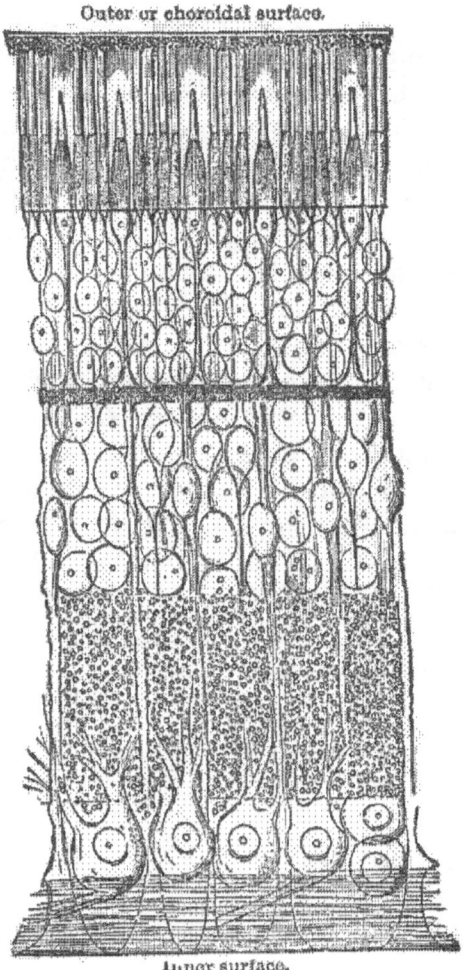

FIG. 65.—Diagrammatic section of Human Retina. (Schultze.)

j, The *Pigment Layer* is the most external part of

the retina. It consists of hexagonal, pigmented epithelial cells, which are prolonged internally into fine filaments that extend between the rods.

The *Retinal Vessels* are comparatively few. They ramify beneath the external limiting membrane and send vessels outward to all the layers as far as the external nuclear one. No vessels are found among the rods and cones or the pigment layer.

7th, The *Lens* is a solid body composed of laminated fibrous material and enclosed in a homogeneous elastic capsule. The lens material, though transparent, is not structureless. It is composed of elongated *Lens Fibres*, running meridionally, and joined together by an interfibrillar cement.

8th, The *Vitreous Humor* is composed of soft gelatinous tissue containing a few scattered cells. It is a mucoid tissue, and is almost the only place where that substance survives in the adult. It fills up the cavity of the eyeball behind the lens.

9th, The *Aqueous Humor* is a clear watery fluid that fills the anterior chamber between the cornea and the lens.

CHAPTER XXI.

The Central Nervous System.

The Spinal Cord.

The Spinal Cord consists of Nerve Cells and Nerve Fibres, with Bloodvessels and Lymphatics; the whole being supported by a connective-tissue framework and surrounded by connective-tissue envelopes. The nerve elements are grouped in a central grayish butterfly-shaped body and a whiter enveloping mass; these are known respectively as the *Gray* and the *White Matter* of the cord. The following structures are found in the organ :

1st, The *Central Canal* is a narrow cylindrical chanel that runs the entire length of the cord. It is situated in the centre of the commissure uniting the two lateral halves of the gray matter; it is composed of delicate connective tissue, and is lined with ciliated epithelium.

2d, The *Neuroglia* is the connective-tissue framework that supports all the structures of the cord. It consists of a delicate network of fibrils imbedded in a homogeneous, transparent semi-fluid matrix, with a number of small, branched, nucleated cells. It is spread throughout the substance of the cord, but is

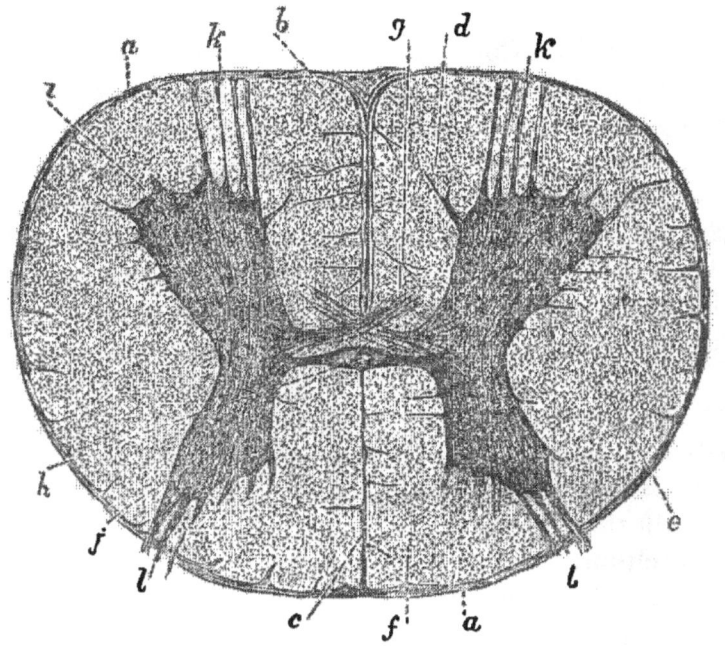

FIG. 66.—Transverse section of Spinal Cord of Calf.

a, Pia Mater. *b*, Prolongation of Pia into Anterior Longitudinal Fissure. *c*, Posterior Longitudinal Fissure. *d*, Anterior column of White Matter. *e*, Lateral column of same. *f*, Posterior column of same. *g*, Anterior White Commissure. *h*, Central Canal. *i*, Anterior Horn of Gray Matter. *j*, Posterior Horn of Gray Matter. *k*, Anterior Nerve Roots. *l*, Posterior Nerve Roots. (Klein.)

greatest in amount between the columns of the cord and at the fissures. Its outermost fibrils are continuous with the connective-tissue envelopes of the cord.

3d, The *Gray Matter* is butterfly-shaped, the body uniting the two wings being called the *Gray Com-*

missure. The lateral masses of gray matter end in the *Anterior* and *Posterior Cornua* or *Horns*, from which spring the spinal nerves. They are composed largely of nerve cells, called *Ganglion Cells*, which are of various shapes, unipolar, bipolar, or multipolar, and branched. Each cell has a large nucleus enclosed in a membrane, in which is a reticulum with one or two nucleoli. The poles of the cells break up into a network of dendritic processes, of which one or two are always thicker than the rest. These are the *Axis-Cylinder Processes*, which sooner or later become invested with a medullary sheath, and become medullated nerve fibres.

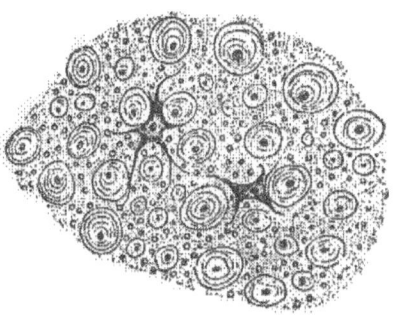

FIG. 67.—From a transverse section of the White Matter of the Cord.

Showing the transversely cut Medullated Nerve Fibres, the Neuroglia between them, with two branched Neuroglia Cells. (Atlas.)

Probably every nerve cell has at least one axis-cylinder process, and is thus directly continuous with a nerve fibre.

Nerve fibres are also found in the gray matter, but not very abundantly. They are largely non-medullated, or are even naked axis-cylinders. Blood and lymph vessels are abundant.

4th, The *White Matter* envelopes the gray matter of the cord completely. It is almost bisected down to the gray commissure by two fissures, known as the *Anterior* and the *Posterior Longitudinal Fissures*. The peculiar shape of the gray matter that it encloses divides it into three distinct portions, the *Anterior*,

Lateral, and *Posterior Columns*. At the bottom of the anterior columns, and just in front of the gray commissure, is a band of fibres, known as the *White Commissure*. The white substance is composed mostly of medullated nerve fibres, but without neurilemmæ. It contains besides blood and lymph vessels the connective tissue of the neuroglia.

5th, The *Pia Mater* is a fibrous connective-tissue membrane lined on both surfaces with a layer of endothelial cells. It closely envelopes the outer surface of the white matter of the cord.

6th, The *Arachnoid* is a delicate connective-tissue network, lined on both sides with endothelial cells. Thus is formed between the arachnoid and the pia the *Sub-Arachnoid Lymph Space*, completely lined, as we have seen, with endothelium.

7th, The *Dura Mater* is the thick outermost membrane that covers the spinal cord. It is composed of several lamellæ of connective tissue with many elastic fibres. It also is lined on both surfaces with endothelium; and the lymphatic space between it and the arachnoid is known as the *Sub-dural Space*.

All three membranes have their own vessels and nerves.

The Brain.

The Brain is composed of nerve elements, supporting connective tissue, vessels, lymphatics, etc., like the cord. Its arrangement is, however, entirely too complicated to be described here. In a general way the organ consists of:

1st, The *Ventricles*, which are cavities similar to and communicating with the central canal of the cord.

THE CENTRAL NERVOUS SYSTEM.

They are lined with a delicate connective tissue and covered with ciliated endothelium. They lie in general in the central gray matter, and form a complicated series of intercommunicating lymphatic spaces.

2d, The *Neuroglia* of the brain is a delicate connective-tissue framework similar to that of the cord. It forms the scaffolding on which the delicate nerve elements and the vessels of the organ are supported.

3d, The *Gray Matter* is collected into a number of masses situated in the interior and at the base of the brain, and called the *Ganglia*, and also spread as a thin layer over the surface of the organ. In it are found the same elements as in the gray matter of the cord—nerve cells of various shapes, with non-medullated nerve fibres, and vessels. Collections of nerve cells in various places form the nuclei of the cranial nerves.

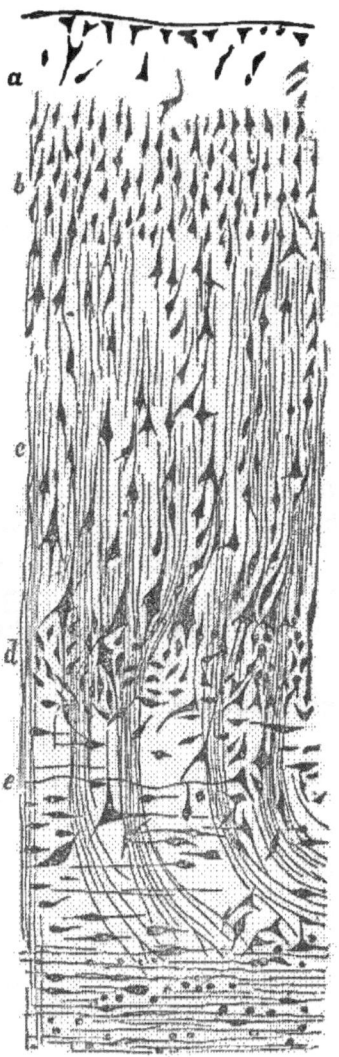

FIG. 68.—Vertical section through the Gray Matter of a Cerebral Convolution.

a, Superficial Layer. *b*, Closely-packed small Ganglion Cells. *d*, Small Multipolar Ganglion Cells. *e*, Spindle-shaped Ganglion Cells. (Meguert.)

4d, The *White Matter* of the brain forms a thick cap enveloping the gangliæ. It is composed of nerve fibres, medullated but without neurilemmæ. They are continuous with the axis-cylinder processes of the cells of the gray matter.

5th, The *Pia Mater* is a connective-tissue membrane, rich in bloodvessels, and closely enveloping the entire surface of the brain. It is lined on both surfaces with endothelium.

6th, The *Arachnoid* is a delicate membrane similar to the pia, and lined like it, with endothelial cells. The *Sub-arachnoid Space* is similar to that of the cord.

7th, The *Dura Mater* is a dense connective tissue and elastic membrane, which differs from the dura of the cord in that it is closely attached to the internal surface of the cranial bones, forming their periostium. It is also lined with epithelium, and a *Sub-dural Space* lies between it and the arachnoid membrane.

The *Bloodvessels* form a dense capillary network throughout the brain; *Lymphatics* also are abundant.

INDEX.

ACINI of Lung,	. 74	BELLINI, Ducts of,	. 102
of Salivary Gland,	. 67	Bile Ducts,	75, 77
Adenoid Tissue,	25, 63	Bladder,	. 104
Adiposus, Paniculus,	. 130	Adventitia of,	. 105
Adventitia,	. 56	Mucosa of,	. 104
of Bladder,	. 105	Muscularis of,	. 104
of Fallopian Tube,	. 117	Nerves of,	. 105
of Ureter,	. 104	Peritoneal Coat of,	. 105
of Urethra,	. 104	Vessels of,	. 105
of Vagina,	. 117	Blood,	. 10
Afferent Vessels of Kidney,	. 108	Composition of,	. 11
Air Cells of Lungs,	. 95	Determination of,	. 13
Albuginea of Testis,	. 106	Granules of,	. 12
Albuminose,	. 3	Red Corpuscles of,	. 10
Albuminous Cells of Salivary		White Corpuscles of,	. 11
Glands,	. 66	Bloodvessels,	. 55
Alimentary Canal,	. 78	Bone,	. 33
Alveoli of Salivary Glands,	. 67	Canaliculæ of,	. 36
Amoeba,	. 5	Cancellous,	. 34
Aqueous Humor,	. 132	Compact,	. 34
Arachnoid of Brain,	. 138	Corpuscles,	. 35
of Cord,	. 136	Development of,	. 38
Arteries, Adventitia of,	. 56	Haversian Canals of,	. 35
Interna of,	. 56	Haversian Systems of,	. 37
Media of,	. 56	Lacunæ of,	. 36
Artery, Hepatic,	75, 77	Lamellæ of,	. 37
Interlobular,	. 102	Ossification of,	. 38
Pulmonary,	. 96	Periostium of,	. 37
Tracheal,	. 96	Bowman's Capsule,	. 99
Renal,	. 102	Sarcous Elements,	. 43
Arytenoid Cartilage,	. 93	Brain, The,	. 136
Auerbach's Plexus,	. 89	Arachnoid of,	. 138
Axis Cylinder,	. 46	Dura Mater of,	. 138
Process,	. 135	Ganglia of,	. 137

INDEX.

	PAGE
Brain, Ganglion Cells of,	135
Gray Matter of,	137
Lymphatics of,	138
Neuroglia of,	137
Pia Mater of,	138
Sub-arachnoid Space of,	138
Sub-dural Space of,	138
Ventricles of,	136
Vessels of,	138
White Matter of,	138
Bronchi,	93
Lymphatics of,	95
Mucosa of,	94
Nerves of,	95
Ultimate,	93
Vessels of,	95
Bronchial Artery,	96
CANAL, Central, of Cord,	133
Canaliculi,	36
Cancellous Bone,	34
Capillaries,	55
Capsule, Bowman's,	99
Glisson's,	75
of Kidney,	99
of Lymphatic Nodes,	65
Cardiac Muscle,	45
Cartilage,	29
Arytenoid,	93
Bronchial,	93
Cricoid,	93
Elastic,	32
Epiglottic,	93
Fibro,	31
Laryngeal,	92
of Santorini,	93
of Wrisberg,	93
Perichondrium of,	29
Thyroid,	93
Cell, The,	1
Cells, Assimilation of,	6
Automatism of,	5
Chief,	85
Constitution of,	1
Duration of,	5
Ganglion,	135
Gustatory,	82
Liver,	74
Metabolism of,	5

	PAGE
Cells, Motion of,	5
Reproduction of,	7
Respiration of,	5
Size of,	4
Cement, the,	78, 80
Ceruminous Glands,	122
Choriocapillaris,	128
Choroid,	128
Lamina Supra-choroidea of,	128
Lamina Vitrea of,	129
Layer of Haller of,	128
Circumvallate Papillæ,	82
Clitoris,	117
Collecting Tubules,	102
Color of Hair,	125
Colostrum,	60
Columns of Cord, Anterior,	136
Lateral,	136
Posterior,	135
Commissure, Gray, of Cord,	134
White, of Cord,	136
Compact Bone,	34
Conjunctiva,	126
Lymphatics of,	126
Nerves of,	126
Connective Tissues,	20
Elastic,	25
Subcutaneous,	121
White Fibrous,	23
Cords, Pulp, of Spleen,	71
Corium,	119
of Mucosæ,	50
Cornea,	128
Anterior Elastic Lamina of,	128
Membrane of Decemet,	128
Posterior Elastic Lamina of,	128
Corneal Tissue,	25
Corneum, Stratum,	119
Cornua, Anterior, of Cord,	135
Posterior, of Cord,	135
Corpora Cavernosa,	110
Corpus Highmori,	106
Luteum,	114
Spongiosum,	110
Corpuscle, Malphigian,	65, 71
Meissner's,	121
Muscle,	44
Nerve,	48
Pacinian,	121

INDEX. 141

	PAGE		PAGE
Corpuscles, Tactile,	80, 121	Epithelium,	15
Cortex of Kidney,	98	Ciliated,	17
Cowper's Gland,	105	Columnar,	16
Cribrosa, Lamina,	128	Gland,	15
Cricoid Cartilage,	98	Pavement,	16
Crusta Petrosa,	8	Eye,	126
Crypts of Lieberkühn,	88	Aqueous Humor of,	132
Cuticle of Hair,	125	Choroid of,	128
Cutis Vera,	119	Conjunctiva of,	126
		Cornea of,	128
DEFERENS, Vas,	110	Iris of,	129
Dentine,	78, 79	Lamina Cribrosa of,	128
Dentinal Fibres,	80	Lens of,	132
Tubules,	80	Retina of,	130
Decemet's Membrane,	128	Sclera of,	126
Development of Bone,	38	Vitreous Humor of,	132
Dilator Pupillæ,	129		
Discus Proligerus,	124	FALLOPIAN Tube,	117
Ducts, Bellini's,	102	Fatty Tissue,	27
Bile,	75, 77	Fibres, Dentinal,	80
Hepatic,	77	Fibro-cartilage,	31
Intralobular,	77	Fibrous Tissue,	23
Dura Mater,	136	Filiform Papillæ,	81
		Follicle, Graafian,	123
EFFERENTES, Vasa,	103	Hair,	122, 123
Elastic Cartilage,	32	Hair, Glassy Membrane of,	124
Connective Tissue,	25	Hair, Hyaline Membrane of	124
Embryonic Connective Tissue,	21	Hair, Papilla of,	124
Enamel,	78	Fungiform Papilla,	82
End Bulbs,	50		
of Glands,	111	GANGLION Cells,	53
Endomysium,	42	Gelatinous Connective Tissue,	21
Endoneurium,	40	Gemmation,	7
Endothelium,	19	Germ Hill,	114
End Plates,	52	Germinal Spot,	114
Epidermis,	118	Vesicle,	114
Horny Layer of,	118	Gland, Prostate,	110
Malphigian Layer of,	119	Thymus,	65
Mucous Layer of,	119	Glands,	63
Rete of,	119	Ceruminous,	122
Stratum Granulosum of,	119	Lymphatic,	63
Stratum Lucidum of,	119	Mucous,	61
Epididymis,	109	of Cowper,	105
Vas Deferens of,	110	of Littré,	105
Vesiculæ Seminales of,	110	of Tongue,	82
Epiglottis,	93	Peptic,	85
Epineurium,	49	Pyloric,	86
Epithelial Layer of Mucous		Sebaceous,	122
Membranes,	50	Solitary,	87

INDEX.

	PAGE		PAGE
Glands, Sudorific,	121	Humor, Vitreous,	132
Sweat,	121	Huxley, Layer of,	125
Glandulæ Uterinæ,	116	Hyaline Coat of Hairs,	124
Glans Penis,	111		
End Bulbs of,	111	INFUNDIBULÆ of Lungs,	95
Papillæ of,	111	Interlobular Artery of Kidney,	102
Glisson's Capsule,	75	Vein of Liver,	76
Glomerulus,	103	Internodal Segment,	48
Goblet Cells,	18	Intestine, Large,	90
Graafian Follicle,	113	Small,	87
Discus Proligerous of,	114	Intima, the,	56
Germ Hill of,	114	Intralobular Vein of Liver,	76
Liquor of,	114	Involuntary Muscle,	40
Membrana Granulosa of,	113	Iris,	120
Theca of,	113	Dilator Pupillæ of,	129
Granulosa, Stratum,	119	Sphincter Pupillæ of,	129
Gray Matter of Brain,	137	Uvea,	129
of Cord,	134		
of Cord, Anterior Cornua of,	134	JUNCTIONAL Tubule,	102
of Cord, Ganglion Cells of,	135		
of Cord, Gray Commissure of,	134	KERATIN,	3
		Kidney,	98
of Cord, Posterior Commissure of,	135	Afferent Arteries of,	103
		Arterial Arches of,	99, 102
Gustatory Cells,	82	Bowman's Capsule of,	99
		Capsule of,	99
HÆMOGLOBIN,	12	Collecting Tubules of,	102
Hair,	122	Convoluted Tubes of,	101, 102
Color of,	125	Cortex of,	98
Cuticle of,	125	Ducts of Bellini of,	102
Fibrous Structure of,	125	Glomerulus of,	103
Follicles of,	122, 123	Henle's Loop of,	101
Lanugo,	123	Interlobular Arteries of,	102
Medulla of,	125	Lymphatics of,	104
Root of,	125	Malphigian Tufts of,	103
Root Sheath of,	125	Medulla of,	98
Shaft of,	125	Nerves of,	104
Tactile,	123	Papillæ of,	98
Haller, Layer of,	128	Renal Artery of,	104
Haversian Canal,	35	Renal Vein of,	104
System,	37	Uriniferous Tubules of,	99
Henle, Layer of,	125	Vasa Recta of,	104
Loop of,	101	Venous Arches of,	99
Hepatic Artery,	75, 77	Vessels of,	102
Ducts,	77	Krause, Membrane of,	44
Vein,	75		
Highmori, Body of,	106	LACUNÆ,	36
Hilum of Lymphatic Glands,	66	Lamellæ,	37
Humor, Aqueous,	132	Lamina, Anterior Elastic,	128

INDEX. 143

	PAGE		PAGE
Lamina, Cribrosa,	128	Lungs, Infundibula of,	95
Posterior Elastic,	128	Lobes of,	95, 96
Supra-choridea,	128	Lobules of,	95, 96
Lanugo Hair,	123	Pulmonary Artery of,	96
Large Intestine,	90	Pulmonary Vein of,	97
Lymphatics of,	91	Vessels of,	95
Mucosa of,	90	Lunula of Nail,	122
Muscularis of,	90	Luschka, Gland of,	65
Nerves of,	91	Luteum, Corpus,	114
Serosa of,	91	Lymph,	14
Submucosa of,	91	Lymphatic Follicles,	63
Vessels of,	91	Glands,	63, 64
Larynx,	92	Nodes,	64, 65
Cartilage of,	92	Sub-arachnoid Space,	136
Lymphatics of,	93	Vessels,	58
Mucosa of,	92	Lymphatics of Brain,	138
Muscles of,	93	of Bronchi,	95
Nerves of,	93	of Cord,	136
Vessels of,	93	of Glands,	66
Layer of Haller,	128	of Glands, Afferent Vessels of	66
Lens,	132	of Glands, Capsule of,	67
Fibres,	132	of Glands, Efferent Vessels of	66
Lieberkühn, Crypts of,	87, 88	of Glands, Hilum of,	66
Liquor Folliculi,	114	of Glands, Lymphatics of,	67
Littré, Glands of,	105	of Glands, Nerves of,	67
Liver,	74	of Glands, Vessels of,	67
Acini of,	74	of Kidney,	104
Bile Ducts of,	75	of Large Intestine,	90
Capsule of,	75	of Skin,	121
Cells of,	74	of Small Intestine,	89
Hepatic Artery of,	75	of Stomach,	87
Hepatic Duct of,	77		
Hepatic Vein of,	75	Malphigian Corpuscles of	
Hilum of,	76	Spleen,	71, 72
Interlobular Vessels of,	77	Malphigian Tufts of Kidney,	99, 103
Intralobular Vessels of,	77	Mammary Gland,	68
Lobules of,	74	Colostrum of,	69
Lymphatics of,	77	Vessels of,	70
Portal Vein of,	76	Marrow,	38
Lobes of Lung,	95, 96	Mater, Dura, of Brain,	138
Lobules of Lung,	95, 96	Dura, of Cord,	136
Longitudinal Fissure, Anterior,		Pia, of Brain,	138
of Cord,	135	Pia, of Cord,	136
Longitudinal Fissure, Posterior,		Matrix of Nails,	122
of Cord,	135	Media, the,	56
Loop of Henle,	101	Medulla of Hair,	125
Lucidum, Stratum,	119	of Kidney,	98
Lungs,	95	Medullary Sheath,	47
Air Cells of,	95	Medullated Nerve Fibres,	46

144   INDEX.

	PAGE		PAGE
Meissner's Corpuscles,	121	Muscle, Unstriped,	40
Plexus,	89	Vessels of,	44
Membrane, Decemet's,	128	Muscularis of Bladder,	104
External Limiting,	131	of Fallopian Tube,	117
Glassy,	124	of Large Intestine,	90
Hyaline,	124	of Œsophagus,	83
Internal Limiting,	131	of Small Intestine,	87
Serous,	61	of Stomach,	87
Serous, Basement Layer of,	61	of Ureter,	104
Serous, Endothelial Layer of,	61	of Urethra,	105
Synovial,	61	of Uterus,	116
Synovial, Basement Layer of,	62	Muscularis Mucosae,	59
Synovial, Endothelial Layer of,	62	of Œsophagus,	83
Synovial, Synovia of,	62	of Small Intestine,	87
Milk,	70	of Stomach,	84
Molecular Layer, External,	130	Papillæ of,	60
Internal,	130	Villi of,	60
Motor Nerve Terminations,	52	NAILS,	122
Mouth,	80	Lunula of,	122
Tactile Corpuscles of,	80	Matrix of,	122
Mucin,	3	Root of,	122
Mucoid Connective Tissue,	21	Nasmyth, Cuticle of,	79
Mucous,	61	Nerve Cell, Layer of Retina,	130
Cells,	66	Cells,	53
Glands,	61	Corpuscles.	48
Mucous Membrane,	59	Nerve Fibres,	46
Corium of,	59	Axis Cylinder of,	46
Glands of,	61	Endoneurium of,	49
Œsophageal,	83	Layer of Retina of,	130
of Bladder,	104	Medulla of,	46
of Fallopian Tube,	117	Medullary Sheath of,	47
of Large Intestine,	90	Neurilemma of,	48
of Larynx,	92	Nodes of,	48
of Small Intestine,	87	Perineurium of,	49
of Stomach,	84	Sheath of Schwann,	48
of Trachea,	93	Nerve Terminations, Motor,	52
of Ureter,	104	Sensory,	50
of Uterus,	116	Nerves of Bronchi,	95
of Vagina,	117	of Cornea,	128
Muscle,	40	of Kidney,	104
Cardiac,	45	of Large Intestine,	91
Corpuscles of,	44	of Larynx,	93
Endomysium of,	42	of Sclera,	128
Nerves of,	44	of Skin,	121
Perimysium of,	42	of Stomach,	87
Sarcolemma of,	42	of Ureter,	105
Sarcous Elements of,	42	of Urethra,	105
Striped,	42	Neuroglia,	25, 54

INDEX. 145

	PAGE		PAGE
Nodes of Ranvier,	48	Perimysium,	42
Lymphatic,	63	Perineurium,	49
Lymphatic, Capsule of,	65	Periostium,	37
Lymphatic, Septa of,	65	Peritoneum,	58
Nuclear Layer of Retina,	130	Peyer's Patches,	65
Nymphæ,	117	Pharyngeal Tonsil of Luschka,	65
		Pia Mater,	136
ODONTOBLASTS,	80	Pigment Cells,	18
Œsophagus,	83	Layer of Retina,	131
External Coat of,	83	Pigmentary Connective Tissue,	25
Internal Coat of,	83	Plasma,	12
Mucosa of,	83	Plates, End,	52
Muscularis of,	83	Pleura,	58, 97
Muscularis Mucosæ of,	83	Plexus, Nerve,	52
Organs, The,	63	of Auerbach,	89
Ossification,	38	of Meissner,	89
Ovary,	112	Portal Vein,	75, 76
Graafian Follicle of,	114	Prickle Cells,	17
Parenchyma of,	112	Prostrate Gland,	110
Stroma of,	112	Pulmonary Artery,	96
Ovum,	114	Vein,	97
Germinal Spot of,	114	Pulp Cords,	71
Germinal Vesicle of,	114	of Spleen,	71
Vitellus of,	114	Pupils, Dilator of,	131
Yolk of,	114	Sphincter of,	129
Zona Pellucida of,	114	Pyloric Glands,	86
PACINIAN Corpuscles,	50, 121	RANVIER, Nodes of,	48
Pancreas,	68	Recta, Vasa,	104
Panniculus Adiposus,	120	Renal Artery,	102
Papillæ of Glans Penis,	111	Vein,	104
of Kidney,	98	Respiratory System,	92
of Mucous Membranes,	50	Rete,	119
of Skin,	118	Malphigi,	119
of Tongue,	81	Mucosa,	119
of Tongue, Filiform,	81	Testis,	107
of Tongue, Fungiform,	82	Reticular Tissue,	24
of Tongue, Circumvallate,	82	Retina,	120
Parietal Cells of Stomach,	85	External Limiting Membrane of,	131
Parotid Gland,	66	External Molecular Layer of,	130
Partition of Krause,	42	External Nuclear Layer of,	130
Patches, of Peyer,	65	Internal Limiting Membrane of,	130
Penis, Corpora Cavernosa of,	110	Internal Molecular Layer of,	130
Corpus Spongiosum of,	110	Internal Nuclear Layer of,	130
End Bulbs of,	111	Layer of Nerve Cells of,	130
Glans,	111	Layer of Nerve Fibres of,	130
Peptic Glands,	85	Layer of Rods and Cones of,	131
Pericardium,	58		
Perichondrium,	29		

INDEX.

	PAGE		PAGE
Retina, Pigment Layer of,	131	Sebaceous Gland of,	122
Vessels of,	131	Sebum of,	122
Rods and Cones, Layer of,	131	Stratum Cornium of,	118
Root of Hair,	125	Stratum Granulosum of,	119
of Nails,	122	Stratum Lucidum of,	119
Root Sheath,	124	Subcutaneous Connective Tissue of,	119
SALIVARY Glands,	66	Sudoriporous, Glands of,	121
Acini of,	67	Sweat Glands of,	121
Albuminous Cells of,	66	Vessels of,	121
Alveoli of,	67	Small Intestine,	87
Mucous Cells of,	66	Leiberkühn's Crypts of,	87, 88
Santorini, Cartilage of,	98	Lymphatics of,	87
Sarcolemma,	42	Mucosa of,	87
Sarcous Elements,	43	Muscularis of,	89
Schwann, Sheath of,	48	Muscularis Mucosae,	87
Sclera,	130	Peyer's Patches of,	87, 89
Nerves of,	126	Serosa of,	89
Vessels of,	126	Solitary Glands of,	87, 89
Sebaceous Glands,	122	Submucosa of,	88
Sebum,	122	Vessels of,	89
Seminal Tubules,	107	Villi of,	87
Seminalis, Vesiculæ,	110	Solitary Glands,	87
Sensory Nerves,	50	Spermatoblasts,	108
Terminations,	50	Spermatozoa,	108
Septa of Lymphatic Nodes,	65	Sphincter Pupillæ,	129
Serosa of Bladder,	105	Spinal Cord,	133
of Large Intestine,	91	Anterior Columns of,	135
of Small Intestine,	89	Anterior Longitudinal Fissure of,	135
of Stomach,	87	Arachnoid of,	136
Serous Membranes,	61	Central Cord of,	133
Sheath of Schwann,	48	Dura Mater of,	136
Sinuses, Lymph,	58, 66	Gray Matter of,	133, 134
Venous, of Spleen,	71	Lateral Columns of,	136
Skin,	118	Neuroglia of,	133
Ceruminous Glands of,	122	Pia Mater of,	136
Corium of,	119	Posterior Columns of,	136
Cutis Vera of,	119	Posterior Longitudinal Fissure of,	135
Epidermis of,	118	Subdural Space of	136
Hair of,	122	Vessels of,	136
Lymphatics of,	121	White Commissure of,	136
Meissner's Corpuscles of,	121	Spleen,	71
Nails of,	122	Capsule of,	73
Nerves of,	121	Malphigian Corpuscles of,	65, 71
Pacinian Bodies of,	121	Pulp of,	71
Panniculus Adiposus of,	120	Venous Sinuses of,	71
Rete of,	119	Spongiosum, Corpus,	110
Rete Malphigi of,	119		
Rete Mucosa of,	119		

INDEX.

	PAGE		PAGE
Stomach,	84	Testis, Rete of,	107
Chief Cells of,	86	Seminal Tubules of,	107
Glands of,	84	Septa of,	106
Lymphatics of,	87	Spermatoblasts of,	108
Mucosa of,	84	Tunica Albuginea of,	106
Muscularis of,	87	Tunica Vaginalis of,	106
Muscularis Mucosa of,	84	Tissues, the,	8
Nerves of,	87	Adenoid,	63
Parietal Cells of,	86	Compound,	55
Peptic Glands of,	85	Contractile,	8
Pyloric Glands of,	86	Irritable,	8
Serosa of,	87	Lymphoid,	63
Submucous Connective		Mechanical,	8
Tissue of,	87	Metabolic,	8
Vessels of,	87	Reproductive,	8
Stomata,	56	Respiratory,	8
Stratum Cornium,	118	Simple,	10
Granulosum,	119	Tongue,	81
Lucidum,	119	Glands of,	82
Striped Muscle,	42	Gustatory Cells of,	82
Subarachnoid Space,	58	Papillæ of,	81
Sublingual Gland,	67	Taste Buds of,	82
Submaxillary Gland,	66	Tonsil, Pharyngeal of Luschka,	65
Substance, White, of Schwann,	47	Tonsils,	65
Sudoriparous Glands,	121	Trachea,	93
Sweat Glands,	121	Cartilages of,	93
Synovia,	62	Mucosa of,	93
Synovial Cavities,	58	Tubules, Collecting,	102
Membranes,	61	Convoluted,	101, 102
		Dentinal,	80
Tactile Corpuscles,	50, 80, 121	Junctional,	102
Hairs,	123	Seminal,	107
Taste Buds,	82	Uriniferous,	99
Teeth,	78	Tube, Fallopian,	117
Cement of,	78, 80	Adventitia of,	117
Crusta Petrosa of,	80	Mucosa of,	117
Cuticle of Nasmyth of,	79	Muscularis of,	117
Dentinal Fibres of,	80	Tufts, Malphigian,	98
Dentinal Tubules of,	80	Tunica Albuginea of,	106
Dentine of,	78, 79	Vaginalis of,	106
Enamel of,	78		
Odontoblasts of,	80	Ultimate Bronchi,	93
Periostium of,	78	Unstriped Muscle,	40
Pulp of,	80	Ureter,	104
Tendon Tissue,	25	Adventitia of,	104
Testis,	106	Mucosa of,	104
Corpus Highmori of,	106	Muscularis of	104
Lobules of,	107	Nerves of,	104
Mediastium of,	106	Vessels of,	104

INDEX.

	PAGE		PAGE
Urethra,	105	Vesicles of Lungs,	95
Adventitia of,	105	Vesiculæ Seminales,	110
Glands of Cowper of,	105	Vessels,	55
Glands of Littré of,	105	Arterial,	56
Lacunæ of,	105	Blood,	55
Mucosa of,	105	Bronchial,	95
Muscularis of,	105	Capillary,	55
Nerves of,	105	Lymphatic,	58
Vessels of,	105	of Bladder,	105
Uriniferous Tubules,	99	of Brain,	138
Uterus,	116	of Cornea,	128
Glandulæ of,	116	of Kidney,	102
Mucosa of,	116	of Large Intestine,	91
Muscularis of,	116	of Larynx,	93
Serosa of,	116	of Retina,	132
Uvea,	129	of Sclera,	128
		of Skin,	121
VACUOLATION,	7	of Small Intestine,	89
Vagina,	117	of Stomach,	87
Adventitia of,	117	of Ureter,	104
Mucosa of,	117	of Urethra,	105
Muscularis of,	117	Venous,	57
Vaginalis, Tunica,	106	Ventricles of Brain,	136
Vas Deferens,	110	Vesticulum,	117
Vasa Afferentes,	103	Villi of Mucosæ,	60
Efferentes,	103	Vitellus,	114
Recta,	104	Vitrea, Lamina,	129
Vasorum,	58	Vitreous Humor,	132
Vein, Hepatic,	75	Voluntary Muscle,	42
Portal,	75, 76		
Pulmonary,	97	WHITE Matter of Brain,	136
Renal,	104	of Cord,	138
Veins,	57	White Substance of Schwann,	47
Interlobular,	77		
Intralobular,	77	YOLK,	114
Sublobular,	77		
Venous Sinuses of Spleen,	71	ZONA Pellucida,	114

www.ingramcontent.com/pod-product-compliance
Lightning Source LLC
Chambersburg PA
CBHW030318170426
43202CB00009B/1060